THE
DAYCROFT
FACTOR

THE DAYCROFT FACTOR

A memoir

"WILLIAM BRUCE" DREDGE

PRIMIX
PUBLISHING
THE WRITE CHOICE

Primix Publishing
East Brunswick Office Evolution
1 Tower Center Boulevard, Ste 1510
East Brunswick, NJ 08816
www.primixpublishing.com
Phone: 1-800-538-5788

Published by Primix Publishing: 01/29/2026

ISBN: 979-8-89194-501-2(sc)
ISBN: 979-8-89194-601-9(hc)
ISBN: 979-8-89194-502-9(e)

Library of Congress Control Number: 2025912014

CONTENTS

DEDICATION

To my wife Judy, our three children Abby, Samantha, and Zachary, their spouses, our seven grandchildren Addisen, Jake, Emmy, Avalise, Callan, Bailey, and Mckenzie; and to all those Truth-seekers who form the cement of our civilization.

FOREWORD

When thinkers of the 20ᵗʰ and early 21ˢᵗ century stop to ponder the factors influencing this time on planet earth, many, if they are honest, justifiably conclude that *something's missing*. Most thinkers come to realize it's not just one thing missing, but rather that we are all largely influenced by our experiences in life, encompassing numerous factors. Some factors are salutary, others, not so much.

During a period of some 55 years spanning three great careers, I have often been led to a recurrent observation: that the moral, ethical, and spiritual elements of our earliest formations often go MIA as the homely succession of sacrifice, work and worldly worry become the wind beneath the wings of the sacrilegious moth of time. Among human beings, not all formations are the same. But it is also true that strong and good formations, which often come to peaceful, prosperous fruitions, are deeply rooted in factors imbedded in them, or gain ascendency during human life's rarely smooth sailing.

Collectively, numerous elements apparent to me have coalesced into a single, multifaceted construct, which it has taken me a half century or more to recognize. Some of its many facets are now recognizable to me by different names, but taken together, I thought its essence worth naming The Daycroft Factor,

CHAPTER 1

Strong Foundations

At the age of five, an ordinary little boy rubbed his sleepy eyes and looked at what his 13-year-old sister and 45-year-old mother had laid out for him on a warm September day in 1951, his first day of school. Nearly everything readied for me was new: new saddle-shoes, new socks, new underwear, new corduroy trousers, new shirt, and the fresh smell of a new leather belt with a cowboy buckle. Making my way to the kitchen, I noticed with delight a new Roy Rogers lunch box, into which my mother was packing a peanut butter and jelly sandwich, crisp carrot sticks, and a thermos of cold milk. Her ever-available smile and helpful encouragement reminded me not to dawdle. Clearly, this was a big day, this first day of school.

It was no ordinary school for this ordinary little boy; and, except for one year in public school in second grade, when my parents chose to abandon life in suburban New York in favor of a lovely country home near Williamsport, Pennsylvania overlooking rolling hills and farmland, it was the only school I had ever attended prior to college.

The Daycroft School was a small private school located for 30 years of its history on 46 beautiful acres near Long-Island Sound in Stamford,

Connecticut. Daycroft was founded in 1928 by a visionary woman, Sara Pyle Smart, who sought to provide early education opportunities for children of parents who were students of Christian Science, then among the fastest-growing religious movements in the United States. While the school had no direct affiliation with the Christian Science church organization, Mrs. Smart chose to provide an educational environment embracing and promulgating the very high moral, ethical, and spiritual precepts and values comprising the genuine doctrine of Christian Science. Over the next several decades, the school grew in popularity, adding to the nursery school established in 1928, and later adding both an elementary school and a college preparatory High School.

It was no short walk across the park to attend Daycroft each day. My older sister Ellie and I would first walk from our home in New Rochelle, NY to the train station nearly a mile away, where we would board a train stopping at Connecticut's Stamford station 18 miles up the New Haven Line, where a school bus would meet us and bring us, along with others who commuted by train to the school. The walk to and from the station was one of those sibling bonding opportunities for Ellie and her little brother - I was seven years younger than she. Arriving at the train platform, Ellie, with a loving big sister smile, would often produce a penny, which she let me insert into a gleaming shiny stainless steel vending machine. She would then allow me to turn the knob - and out would come a package of two Chicklets chewing gum, which I would share with her. The memories of a big sister's love, undimmed by the sights, sounds and smells of trains, distant train whistles, and train stations, formed a fond appreciation of them throughout my adulthood. My daily walks with Ellie, I suspect, incubated a very deep affection and respect for the female of the species.

Mothers such as ours regarded the Daycroft School as a veritable pedagogical oasis in what they viewed as the materialistic jungle of public-school education which was emerging in post World War two metropolitan and suburban areas. Daycroft was for them the perfect place to send their children to learn academics, in a protected moral environment free from the "progressive" indoctrination and growing crass materialism of the era. It was to them well worth any financial sacrifices entailed. My own parents sacrificed mightily to pay for the Daycroft experience. It was important to Daycroft parents that their children learn to "come out from among them, and be separate" in the words of Saint Paul, found in his second epistle to the Corinthians. No sense of condescension in this desire and intention was recognized by the young children. That conflict would later begin to emerge during adolescence.

My oldest sister, Beverly, was 13 years older than I, five years older than my sister Ellie, and had attended New Rochelle High School when I was a toddler. She and my mother were routinely observed screaming at each other, with my father barely able to mediate between them. A legal drinking age of 18 at the time, teenagers smoking cigarettes, relaxed boundaries of behavior, and mediocre academic standards all seemed to represent an increasingly permissive society - even a fashionable one; rarely but occasionally a teenage girl would find herself pregnant, then forced to give her child up for adoption, sometimes under the cruelest and most traumatic circumstances. It drove my mother, daughter of Irish immigrants, orphaned at age seven, straight up the proverbial wall. The bitter strife in our home was constant until Beverly eloped shortly after graduating from New Rochelle High School with a handsome Irish Catholic boy from a family of considerable means; both families were unhappy with the situation.

The faculty of the Daycroft School came to be what one might expect of a small private college preparatory school in mid-20th century New England. Faculty included graduates of highly reputable colleges, holding advanced degrees in their areas of expertise from educational powerhouses such as Harvard, Columbia, New York University, and others. Graduates of tiny Principia College in Elsah, Illinois, founded in 1912 by Mary Kimball Morgan, also had a marked presence on Daycroft's faculty. Mary Kimball Morgan was the daughter of J.P. Morgan. Her stated purpose in founding Principia was to "serve the cause of Christian Science". Combined with very high academic standards, Principia's mission seemed a natural fit for Daycroft faculty.

Daycroft faculty members, seeking to emphasize the mutual blessings of compassion and respect, taught students not to stand in judgment of others. My mother, orphaned at age seven, revered that ethic. However, informed by unpleasant circumstances of her own childhood, involving the darker side of corruption within the Roman Catholic Church, she sometimes honored it in the breach. Class distinctions at Daycroft were made in other ways, mostly among students of High School age. On balance, moral and ethical motives and acts were key elements of what I call "The Daycroft Factor" taught as early as in the Foundation School, first imparted to kindergartners, to whom acceptance of others normally comes quite naturally.

Two of the main buildings at the Stamford Campus were previously enormous pre-WWII manor homes, called Hill House and Adelaide Hall, which separately housed boys' and girls' dormitories, dining facilities, and administrative offices. One of these mansions, Adelaide Hall, had been purchased from the Louis H. Porter Estate during the 1935-1936 school year. A decade later, Mrs. Smart's vision led her to acquire the elegant Hill House property, separated from Adelaide Hall only by a quiet country lane, Blakely Road, which provided public access to the school. Hill House housed elementary school classrooms on its first floor for day students up to sixth grade; its upper two floors housed the boy's dormitory. Both Hill House and Adelaide Hall also featured very large, elegant libraries, which sometimes served as open-architecture impromptu classrooms in the 1950s. Spacious and illuminated with abundant natural light from a long expanse of French doors overlooking an enormous terrace and sweeping campus views of ball fields and open meadows, Adelaide Hall's library was large enough for dance and cotillion classes. It also accommodated music classes, and the entire Daycroft Chorus's performances. The chorus's Christmas performances were often recorded by local radio stations, with copies available for purchase by friends and family, and the public at large.

The main High School academic building, nicknamed "the A-Building", was a converted and enlarged greenhouse located a short walk from Hill House. When previously privately owned, all manner of produce and flora flourished there; after alterations it contained a dozen well-lit classrooms, and a large student entry foyer and locker area where the original greenhouse glass had been retained, providing warmth and light on even the cloudiest days; classrooms had enormous greenhouse glass windows providing abundant natural light and warmth in the cold New England Autumn, Winter and Spring seasons when school was in session. Built into the hill from which Hill House derived its name, the A-building was energy-efficient as well as utilitarian, sitting atop an enormous basement, which had formerly been a large storage and carriage area, accessible by cars and delivery vehicles; it also featured a woodshop and ancillary spaces augmenting a comprehensive educational experience.

A row of hedges along a berm separated the A-building from a half-acre of formal gardens, complete with wading pool and fountain; from the garden rose wide beveled slate steps to a gravel walkway leading to the rear terraces of Hill House. Replete with a variety of flora, the garden represented an unmistakable quality of thoughtful planning, and a deep respect for ecology. Weather permitting in June, the High School graduation ceremony was held there, during which each individual graduate made the long-awaited and well-earned walk, with Pomp and Circumstance accompaniment, from the gardens to one of Hill House's several terraces, where graduate candidates, school officials, and prominent keynote speakers were seated. Graduation at the Stamford campus was a poignantly touching ceremony, well suited for a graduating class of generally fewer than 50 students.

The Daycroft elementary school was all for which a little boy's or girl's parents could ask: loving, caring teachers and helpers who adored the little ones, and provided a classical age-appropriate education in which children as young as five were taught the joys of reading, basic arithmetical and geometrical concepts, and introduction to foreign languages. Kindergartners had nap time after lunch. Mats and blankets were arranged by the students themselves, spaced eight feet apart on the floor of a large open classroom. Stuffed animals, coloring books, and quiet activities were allowed, including the building of little structures made with finely sanded wooden boards and building blocks; only needed conversation was allowed. French doors led to a small fenced-in play area outside, big enough for kindergartners to move about freely. There was a low see-saw, some low gym bars suitable for exercising little limbs, and a few large converted wooden dog houses with shingled roofs suitable for little people to play house, even on rainy days.

Physical education began in kindergarten, with swimming lessons at the local Stamford YMCA; and, beginning in 5th grade, an arrangement was made with that organization for activities involving gymnastics, including a large regulation-sized trampoline, and various running activities on an elevated indoor track during winter. The large trampoline helped students learn the mechanics, balance and safety requirements for gymnastics, with rudimentary tumbling, vaulting, and rings lessons a regular part of the YMCA-run program. Supervised outdoor daily recess sessions on large open fields adjacent to Hill House, featuring jungle gyms and other sturdy playground equipment of an age-appropriate variety rounded out the physical education curriculum at the youngest ages. No separate physical education classes were offered at the older ages, because every child had the opportunity and responsibility to participate in one or more of Daycroft's seasonal sports teams.

Well-planned field trips to local manufacturing, agricultural, and banking institutions provided a varied introductory foundation to the world into which these students would someday enter. The Daycroft elementary school was in fact called The Foundation School. Palpable nurturing and guidance supported visionary educational development, along with regular visits to New York City's art museums, opera houses, symphony halls, and planetariums, all of which added value to a student's earliest educational foundation.

Each grade level advanced appropriately in the accoutrements of formal education, honing reading and math skills, learning to sit quietly while listening to and participating in well-planned and usually well-presented lessons. Practical sciences involved studying things like caterpillars becoming butterflies, or cocoons hosting praying mantis (which hatched one spring day in my first-grade classroom, causing memorable hilarious pandemonium). Observations of bird migratory patterns on campus, kittens and puppies gestated and born, cursive writing, neat printing, the use of compasses, protractors, stencils, and such other formative foundational tools children through grade school could be expected to handle in the 1950's were all staples of the Daycroft Foundation School experience.

During fifth grade, I was requested by Ruth White, a remarkable teacher, to occasionally help a very bright, good-natured boy, who had a full head of carrot-colored hair, was quite friendly, and could make people laugh. Timothy, whom we as classmates knew as "Timmy", wore extremely thick eyeglasses, and was sometimes driven to school in a limousine, accompanied often by his beautiful red-haired mother. Part of my requested assignment was to walk with him on the Stamford YMCA's elevated track during physical education classes there, staying alert to help him avoid any potential dangers, such as steps or other obstacles. Once, while walking with me on the elevated track, Timmy said he needed to stop for a moment to rest, and suggested I run around the entire track for exercise. He added that he would time me, promising that he would hold the handrail until I returned. The thoughtfulness of that gesture exemplified what the Foundation School instilled. I did my best Roger Banister imitation and sprinted around the track, arriving back beside Timmy, winded. The humor in Timmy's comment, that he had forgotten his stopwatch but had counted to 76, was not lost on me. We were 10 years old at the time.

Timmy's mother, a student of Chrisitan Science, was the fifth wife of billionaire J.P. Getty. She had sent Timmy to The Daycroft School knowing he would not be judged, nor teased, nor neglected in any way. Her confidence was well warranted and rewarded. Near the end of the school year, Timmy had asked his parents if he could have a pool party at their exquisite country home, which his parents arranged. Most students invited had little if any adult awareness of financial wealth at that time. However, we were reminded that the party invitation was an opportunity to enjoy a special treat, express gratitude, courtesy and good manners. As we were leaving, we were introduced to a man who was wearing a suit and tie, but was quite cordial. When it was my turn, I thanked him and Timmy's mother for the party, adding a ten-year-old's honest appraisal of their beautiful home. The gracious response was a simple but sincere, "We're very happy you enjoyed it".

The difference between the rather humble abode in which I lived, and the spectacularly large and beautiful mansion property in which my friend Timmy lived, was more seen than felt following that very brief conversation, which capped a delightful experience. After all, Timmy's was a huge house set on a beautiful property with a large swimming pool, tennis courts, and the rest; but I had a public golf course across the street from my parents' home, the Rippowam River some 200 yards away to swim in, nearby woods in which to explore and play various games, Hubbard Heights Park a short bike ride away with public tennis courts and ballfields ... and two eyes to help navigate my way to and among all these things. No sense of covetousness plagued my young consciousness – an important aspect of Daycroft's pedagogy, which embraced the tenets of the Hebrew Decalogue. Several years later, I learned the sad news that my friend Timmy had been diagnosed with a brain tumor, resulting in his passing in 1958 following several surgical operations attempting to save his life.

The athletic facilities on Daycroft's campus were mostly geared toward field sports and tennis. Separate regulation soccer, American football, baseball, and field-hockey fields were generally well-groomed natural turf, complemented by adjoining practice areas, designed to keep game fields pristine for competitive inter-scholastic events. The gymnasium and locker rooms were in a large converted horse stables/ barn complex. The basketball court itself was regulation-sized, but with a very narrow border between the edge of the court and walls on three sides, and perhaps six feet on the side leading to an equipment storage room and entrance into the shower room and lockers. It was a barely adequate facility. The basketball court itself was in good condition, evidently seen as suitable for the girls' basketball team's home court. Women's basketball at the time was restricted and slow- moving compared with the men's game, with rules designed to limit full-court running. The Daycroft Varsity men's basketball team's practices and home games were played at the local National Guard armory in downtown Stamford.

In 1963, a decision was made to sell the Stamford campus and relocate to what was thought to be a more suitable and prestigious location in Greenwich, Connecticut. In addition to the perceived financial advantages of "downsizing" to a smaller campus, another reason given to students' families for selling the Stamford campus reflected a certain level of effete class-consciousness: the surrounding residential area was becoming inhabited by "undesirable elements", including juvenile miscreants who were said to harass students living on campus during the school year, and vandalize the school during the summer months. In retrospect, this assessment represented a departure from the ideals which had previously drawn many parents and students to Daycroft, of outreach and inclusivity designed to elevate consciousness. It seemed to contradict the school's motto - "Perceive, then Demonstrate". Rather than take a stand with the strong morals and ethics of Christian Science, it had the appearance of cowardly expedience. It was an early manifestation of a recidivism that many years later I had the opportunity to witness firsthand, professionally. "Dear Lord, please don't let them find me" seemed to be a silent prayer Christian Scientists who lacked the courage of their convictions might pray. Happy to partake of the fruits of others' earlier sacrifices, particularly the wealth and prestige associated with the early successes of Christian Science, the move seemed to expose the desire to circle the wagons, wrap the Spirit of Christian Science in the graveclothes of wealth and exclusivity, and to "light a candle, and put it under a bushel", as Saint Matthew put it. It seemed to be a mindset which grew more prevalent throughout the Boston-based Christian Science Church organization over the ensuing thirty years, which I would witness first-hand while performing professional services there betweem 1989 and 1992. Increasingly, the Christian Science movement was becoming an exclusive club: "Club C.S. "

In fairness, local teenage motorists did occasionally drive onto the Daycroft campus and harass students. I witnessed this one Saturday afternoon in my junior year, while on campus waiting outside Adelaide Hall to rendezvous with my day-student girlfriend. A lovely neighbor of hers who was driving the car bringing them to our rendezvous had reportedly signaled the universal digital salute to some local hooligans, affectionately then known as "greasers", who had followed her onto the campus. As the girls hurried inside, I approached the hooligans' car, asking them if they were lost. Their response was caustic, vituperative, vulgar and threatening, suggesting in lurid detail what they wanted to do with the two "bitches" they had followed. There were four of them in the car; and so, I tried to kill time while reasoning with them, advising them that they were on private property, that they were trespassing, that I had their license plate number, and that my brother-in-law was a police detective in town (actually my brother-in-law's brother-in-law, Josh Healy). Relief arrived when a no-nonsense, muscular, older football teammate appeared, coming to study in the Adelaide Hall library with his girlfriend. As I sardonically explained to him what these locals said they wanted to do, my teammate kicked the side of their car hard, then immediately growled "get the hell out of here "; whereupon they sped off, universal digital salutes flying out the windows, the intruders shouting that they would be back.

Many years later, the justification for the decision to sell and move the school was revised to suggest that "industry had caught up with Daycroft". That deft bit of revisionism ignored the fact that as early as 1957, led by a forward-thinking educator, Headmaster James Heggie, the intention to continue at the Stamford campus had been advanced. Heggie had circulated architectural renderings to parents and other supporters of a modern multi-story building, to be built on the campus's abundant open space to accommodate the school's *intended growth*. Regardless, the decision to sell the property and downsize was a decision from which the school, as such, would never recover. The Stamford campus was in fact soon purchased by Clairol, Inc for a fraction of the price it would fetch today. The graceful, magnificent manor buildings on the bucolic campus were subsequently razed, becoming but a source of fond memories for former students who were privileged to live and be educated in them.

The college preparatory school was largely a co-ed boarding school, with separate boy's and girl's dormitories, where children from all over The United States and other parts of the world lived during the school year. Many students also commuted from homes within a 50-mile radius of the school, some from New York City. The elementary and middle schools accommodated day-students only. One of my friends, at the age of 6, rode a subway from Brooklyn to New York's Grand Central Station every day, accompanied by an adult. Once on the train to Stamford, older schoolmates kept an eye on him. One seventh grader often rode his bike the six miles on busy U.S. Route 1 from nearby Cos Cob, Connecticut to Daycroft's Stamford campus. One 5th grader, a brilliant little wizard of a 10-year-old, actually converted a child's metal pedal car from foot power to battery power, and regularly motored himself along the sidewalk bordering Blakeley Road to classes. He was clearly "too cool for school" - long before Elon Musk became a household name.

Daycroft had instituted a comportment/deportment point system, developed to instill thoughtful behavior every moment of every day throughout the school year. Beginning in 7th grade, each student was required on Fridays to review a five by seven-inch index card, which was kept in a card file accessible to both students and faculty. This card contained entries reflecting the faculty's anonymous assessments of a student's behavior throughout the week. A point system tabulation placed students into groups, listed "A" (highest) through "E" (lowest). A low comportment/deportment score resulted in penalty consequences - for high school boarding students, restriction to campus, or even to one's room during free time - for day students, notes to parents and exclusion from on-campus social activities. Proof that a student had been drinking or smoking was grounds for immediate suspension, and reports of such activity were sternly investigated. One grouping, marked in red pencil – "Red-E Group" – was tantamount to probation, warning the possibility of expulsion.

Upper school boys and girls found engaging in overt public displays of affection such as kissing on campus, or off, were warned and otherwise entreated not to succumb to their animal instincts. College-bound students were encouraged not to allow mere physical attraction to impel their motives and acts when considering marriage. By today's standards, the educational environment might seem harsh and repressive. A competing view was that this environment was well-disciplined, guided by very strong ideals, and designed to instill the ethical and moral standards of Christian Science at the earliest ages, including respect for those of the opposite sex. In those days, deviation from the gender norms of male and female was essentially unknown outside of arcane medical studies. Masculinity and femininity were presented as being *elements of thought, not simply physique.*

The Daycroft School also sought to instill appreciation and respect for many different world cultures prevailing before and during the Cold War of the 1950s. Toward the end of each school year, usually May or early June, the entire student body - from kindergartners to High School Seniors – celebrated International Day, featuring a day's celebration of music, dance, food, and cultural activities from around the world, followed by a student-faculty softball game, other field events, and barbeque. The school's chorus and students from different countries made important contributions to International Day. Daycroft's faculty tried to instill the view that America's emergence from WWII as the preeminent economic engine of the world, was built on a moral construct which welcomed and respected all cultures. This view had not yet morphed into the globalism of the 21st century. In addition to the National Anthem, Jean Sibelius's "Finlandia" was sung in unison by the entire student body and faculty on International Day; as were all verses of the patriotic "This is my Country", written by Al Jacobs and Don Raye in 1940. Tears of joy and hope were common among parents and visitors during these renditions, many of whom had known the horrors of war, and as a result deeply wanted peace in the world for their children. It was an annual ritual at the end of the school year from which strong and lasting foundational memories were made.

Some 30 years later, a decade or so after President Richard Nixon severed the last vestige of financial order in the world, I came face-to-face with how Daycroft's noble efforts to teach the value of divine, unconditional, efficacious love, compassion, and tolerance as a worldview had morphed into what I have more recently come to call "globaloney".

Serving as both president of the South Brunswick Soccer Club and on the Township's Recreation Advisory Board in the 1980s, I thought it educationally useful to name the Township in-town recreational soccer teams alphabetically, by country. An irate parent had written a letter to the Soccer Club, copied to the local paper, that his child "will NEVER play on a team named Cuba! ". Happily, the private travelling teams the soccer club sponsored were named according to astronomical science. The one I coached with a winning record was The Constellation.

Perhaps it was the smaller class sizes at The Daycroft School;

perhaps it was the slower, more deliberate, thorough, and gentler way of teaching very young students, meeting their educational needs individually; perhaps it was the alertness to a five-year-old's fear of the water during swim classes, allayed by the strong, kind, fatherly way the bearded swim instructor, Mr. Gunther, coaxed me into the water, guaranteeing support, providing it, and showering me with praise as progress was made, causing me to look forward to swim day; perhaps it was being turned loose in an enormous meadow at recess to run and play tag, to climb the jungle-gym, to learn the pecking orders children learn when they are allowed to choose their own teams for baseball or hide-and-seek or various other games, all under the watchful eye of teachers who were kind and alert to danger, including bullying; perhaps it was a combination of all these things, and much more; but whatever it was, it built a very strong foundation. Parents were encouraged to visit at any time, unannounced, and participate in class activities, with a condition of visit that each child was to be respected, whether or not his or her parents could be there for any reason. Parental involvement was both cherished and expected at Daycroft. The "Dad's Club" and "Mother's Club" were not simply fund-raisers, although fund-raise they did. There were also orientation and seminar classes for parents, in which the ethics and morals which the school attempted to instill at the very earliest ages were reviewed and emphasized.

CHAPTER 2

Modern Medicine's Meandering March

The Daycroft School was not without some controversy. One of the more distinguishable controversial aspects, which might be regarded as appalling by today's standards, was the school's generally not paying much attention to *materia medica* – Latin, meaning "material medicine" - what we usually today call modern medicine. This departure from prevailing school administration was primarily based on a curious, and at times unfortunate combination of circumstances. First, there was the misunderstanding and/or misapplication, including by many students and teachers of Christian Science, of the teachings of its discoverer and Founder, Mary Baker Eddy, regarding *materia medica*. Second, there were both slow progress and glaring inconsistencies within the healthcare profession in the 1950s. It was not uncommon at that time to observe physicians, dentists and nurses smoking cigarettes, even in their workplaces. Television tobacco advertisers even stooped occasionally to depicting a fictitious Doctor favoring their brand. Surgeons, mostly male, routinely performed questionably necessary, and sometimes outright unnecessary hysterectomies. Drugs such as Thalidomide were prescribed and taken, often with tragic results, before removal from the market. Third, there was a tendency on the part of even very well-educated Chrisitan Scientists to allow "nature to run its course."

Unlike most public schools at the time, The Daycroft School did not require vaccinations as a condition of attendance. In fact, in the midst of a 1959 polio epidemic, the Connecticut State Legislature voted to allow religious exemptions from vaccinations, for which some parents opted. For parents (and faculty), not all of whom were practicing Christian Scientists, this presented questions among those deeply supportive of the morals and ethics of Christian Science benefitting their children, and those equally or more concerned for their children's health. To complicate matters, Daycroft was not a religious school, having no direct or official affiliation with what the public regarded as "The Christian Science Church", which surreptitiously discouraged medical treatment at that time. The conflicts could be daunting for parents of Daycroft students, and somewhat confusingly embarrassing for the students themselves. Once, as I was sleigh-riding on a hill across the street from our home with some friends from school, a youngster whom we didn't know collided with the sled of another child, who suffered a nasty head laceration, which was bleeding. An adult on the scene asked me as to who lived in the neighborhood and might know of a doctor. Stammering, I offered sheepishly, "we're Christian Scientists", my friend quickly adding "we don't go to doctors". The incredulous look on the man's face was not atypical. He walked the boy toward adjacent Bridge Street.

While the consequences of bad economic and monetary policies caused numerous private schools to close, or merge their operations with other private schools, it was in all likelihood the reputation for eschewing modern medicine which presented the biggest enrollment challenges to The Daycroft School over time. Many parents unfamiliar with the actual writings and teachings of Mary Baker Eddy regarding medical treatment were not aware of the ways in which her teachings had, since her passing in 1910, come to be misrepresented by "Christian Science Church" governance.

As a result, some parents, otherwise enamored with the moral and ethical aspects of Daycroft's environment, had understandable cause for pause regarding how situations requiring medical attention would be addressed.

Mary Baker Eddy had made clear in her writings her very visionary view that science would evolve beneficially over time, as would what she praised as "the nobler class of physician". Indeed, her views regarding *all* science, reflecting the noteworthy advances of the Scientific Revolution between the 16th and 18th centuries, were quite prescient. Mrs. Eddy was also very clear as to what practical therapeutic steps her followers should take, given the medical limitations of the 19th century, when the need arose. For example, in a chapter of her seminal book Science and Health, with Key to the Scriptures, first published in 1875, she instructed that, "it is better for Christian Scientists to leave surgery and the adjustment of broken bones and dislocations to the fingers of a surgeon"; in another chapter, entitled "Teaching Christian Science" there is instruction that if prayerful assistance from another Christian Scientist doesn't bring relief, "God will still guide them into the right use of temporary and eternal means"; other examples abound in her other writings. If these instructions were understood, they were apparently not well promulgated by the governance of the First Church of Christ Scientist, in Boston Massachusetts, which surreptitiously eschewed medical treatment.

In 1992, I was invited to attend an investment research seminar on healthcare and healthcare insurance at New York City's Waldorf Astoria, which provided, along with healthcare investment issues, some historical perspective on the question "to doctor, or not to doctor". The late U.S. Senator Daniel Patrick Moynahan was the keynote speaker, perhaps chosen to bolster then-First Lady Hillary Clinton's health insurance initiatives. A dynamic orator, the Senator posed the question, "Who here would have gone to a hospital in 1864"? A couple of analysts in the front row politely raised their hands; whereupon Mr. Moynahan, with characteristic erudite aplomb, walked over to them, lowered his face to theirs, and emphatically declared, "NOOOO! THEY KILLED PEOPLE!", which brought peals of laughter from the attendees, acknowledging the great Senator's perspicacity. Along with the works of Deepak Chopra published in the 1980s and 1990's, it greatly clarified my own conclusions about the prescience of Mrs. Eddy's teachings on the subject of health and healthcare.

There were other questionable deviations from what Mrs. Eddy taught at the end of the 19th century and the beginning of the 20th, one of which has the markings of devious motives. A subtle altering of Mrs. Eddy's Church Manual announced to the press *immediately* upon her passing in 1910 has been called into question by various scholars, including the late noted historian Dr. Rolf Swensen, a Daycroft alumnus, class of 1963. Rolf earned his Ph.D. in synthetic organic chemistry from Cornell, and later distinguished himself in his postdoctoral research in chemistry and imaging probe development at the University of Geneva in Switzerland, and the University of Wisconsin-Madison. However, Rolf also made major contributions to historical scholarship with several works on the history of the Christian Science Movement, including a book published shortly after his passing in 2025 entitled And O'er Earth's Troubled Angry Sea.

Largely unknown to many, in 1919 The Board of Directors of The Mother Church, The First Church of Christ, Scientist, in Boston, Massachusetts had brought suit in Massachusetts to gain control of the Christian Science Publishing Society. Mrs. Eddy, in her *original* Church Manual had given autonomy to The Christian Science Publishing Society, with specific instructions that it turn over its profits (*not its losses*) to the Church twice per year. Her foresight appears wisely intended to prevent putting the church in the position of having to subsidize future operations of the Publishing Society. The wisdom of her vision was made manifest more than a half century later, when the venerable Christian Science Monitor, a non-religious publication struggling to compete as a profitable newspaper, forced the church to heavily support this otherwise highly respected international daily newspaper financially.

As has happened to other religious institutions from time immemorial, the spiritual gyroscope identifying and inherited from this inspired thinker's ministry was thrown out of balance after Mrs. Eddy died. Confusing and deceiving the public, including many Christian Scientists, regarding Mrs. Eddy's views on the medical issue, helped sow the seeds of the Boston church's gradual decline of beneficial influence. The 1919 - 1921 litigation, referred to as The Great Litigation in scholarly circles, became one of the obscured stories of the Christian Science movement, and a veiled dispositive event for those who became interested in Christian Science.

It wasn't until 1972 that confusion over the medical issue came home to roost at Daycroft. In that year, an outbreak of poliomyelitis temporarily closed the school, exacerbating the confusion, once again drawing popular attention to the medical issue. Within 20 years the school's enrollment had dwindled to numbers that made its continuation as a traditional elementary and secondary school unsustainable. In 1990, while a journalist, I was interviewing a Specialist on the floor of the New York Stock Exchange, who happened to live near the Daycroft School's Greenwich campus. Intrigued by learning of Monitor Television's role as the non-religious broadcasting publication of the venerable Christian Science Monitor, he exclaimed that Christian Science was the "world's largest reservoir of polio myelitis".

The Daycroft School closed its doors as a school in the early 1990s, amid desperate efforts including selling off seven-and-a-half acres of the Greenwich campus land, which compromised zoning ordinances, making a sale difficult. Opportunistic investment managers, members of the Christian Science church, subsequently formed a 501c3 Foundation bearing the school's name, which used proceeds of the eventual sale to help fund a charity providing grants to organizations operating at the periphery of The Christian Science Church, including summer camps. It has also embarked on educational projects abroad.

With the exception of my birth, and in connection with the required vaccinations to attend a Williamsport, Pa. public elementary school in second grade, I had never been examined by a medical doctor until 1962, when New York State required a physical exam in connection with my application for working papers at age 16. Chicken Pox and other childhood maladies had been compliantly navigated by my mother, who had become a student of Chrisitan Science a few years prior to my birth. My father, a highly educated Presbyterian immigrant from Canada, was a supporter of his wife's mostly sensible approach to making prayerful consideration of these things a priority. However, as I would be grateful to learn in my late 'teens, my dad would sometimes assert decision-making authority when he felt medical treatment would have to share the stage with metaphysical treatment for his children, a view rejected by many Christian Science Practitioners listed in the Christian Science Journal at that time, and often since.

The view that Christian Science should not be mixed with medical treatment came into clear international focus beginning in 1988, when two parents, David and Ginger Twitchell, reported to be devout Chrisitan Scientists, were charged with involuntary manslaughter in connection with the death of their two-year old son, Robyn. The State of Massachusetts brought suit against the two church members, charging that Robyn had died of the consequences of peritonitis caused by a perforation of the child's bowel, which had been obstructed as the result of an anomaly known as Meckel's diverticulum. The child suffered for five days under the care of a Christian Science Practitioner, without medical help. The State successfully argued that the condition *could have been* treated by surgery with a high success rate. The child had died on April 8th, 1986. There had previously been litigation surrounding other juvenile deaths associated with relying on Christian Science treatment, with claims of First Amendment rights vs the compelling duty of the state to protect children, among other legal arguments presented. The conviction of the Twitchells was a clear signal to me that the church must correct the ambivalence previously presented to its members on the subject, or lose any support I might provide. This presented a conflict for me, because I was engaged by them to do on-air television work at the time. Adding further consternation was a major constitutional issue: after reading news reports that when the child actress Heather O 'Rourke died two years after the Twitchells were charged, following surgery for a bowel obstruction, I learned her parents were not similarly charged. To me, that did not square with the Equal Protection Clause of the 14th Amendment of the U.S. Constitution, about which rule of law students at The Daycroft School were required to learn some thirty years before.

It took perhaps another thirty years after that for The Daycroft Factor to again influence how I view the medical issue. The specter of vaccinations machinations moved front and center in connection with the Covid-19 pandemic. Since Sir Francis Bacon's <u>Novum Organum</u>, published in 1620 during the so-called Scientific Revolution, scientists in the continuum of medical science had begun to theorize that by becoming vaccinated, a body develops immunity from various diseases, both bacterial and viral, including those deemed contagious. Tested over hundreds of years, this theorization has established consensus, and the use of data accumulated as a result, warrants merit. The process of inoculation, which introduces a disease antigen into an organism such as a plant or human body for the purpose of producing antibodies resistant to that disease is now settled medical science.

The popular Sailor's ditty of Irish origin during the 1870's, "What Shall we do with the Drunken Sailor", the lyrical response to which prescribes "Give 'em a hair of the Dog that Bit 'em" helped the public understand the medical theory of *similia similibus curator* – Like cures Like – illustrating the scientific theory of vaccination and inoculation.

It was at one time believed that a hair ingested or placed on the bite wound made by a rabid dog would cure rabies. Simply put – *a little bit of the cause can cure the effect*. Unfortunately, in the case of rabid dog bites, only mythology and learned quackery, not data, supported that theory.

It had taken the 1798 observations of British Scientist Edward Jenner, who noticed that farmers who contracted cowpox were immune to smallpox, to initiate the study of viruses, which resulted in an effective vaccine for smallpox. However, it wasn't until Louis Pasteur's use of the Scientific Method theorized in 1880 that certain bacteria caused disease. Pasteur's pathogen of choice to study: *rabies*, which was actually a virus. In 1892, also using the Scientific Method, Dmitri Ivanovsky discovered that diseased tobacco plants contained a substance infectious to healthy tobacco plants. Co-discoverer Martinus Beijernick called the living infectious fluid "a virus". The Daycroft Factor reminded me that Mary Baker Eddy had published her writings during the same period that other inspired thinkers, including Pasteur, were publishing theirs.

Today, a two-dose injection of human rabies immune globulin will prevent someone bitten by a rabid dog from being one of the 50,000 humans killed world-wide each year by rabid dogs. Four doses after such a bite within two weeks of the bite will cure it. The difference between "Hair of the Dog" therapy and human rabies immune globulin protocols is found in one word : "data". For over a century, medical science has used data as a basis for calculations to determine statistical risk and reward. Not a guarantee of a cure, but a useful metric representing desire and intent. Other vaccines, notably against poliomyelitis, measles, mumps, rubella and other diseases have been shown *by data* to prevent or slow the spread of those diseases. Every single time ? No. Anecdotes and one-off reports of adverse impacts exist, but are statistically rare, and can involve other factors. However, the longer the data stream of consistent positive results consistent with fewer negative results, the more effective a vaccine containing a live virus antigen is trusted.

That fact collided with The Daycroft Factor during the calamitous events of the Pandemic between 2020 and 2023. I observed that given the choice, most caring individuals *wanted* to "trust the science"; but, *there wasn't any*, or not enough upon which both reasonable medical and non medical people could make thoroughly informed choices. Also in conflict with the Daycroft Factor : the right of informed choice itself was being challenged, because our systems of health were more or less being governed by our thinking about systems of pharmacy, and largely still are. I was reminded by a bit of humorous irony at the time that the word "pharmacy" is derived from the Greek word *pharmakon,* which intriguingly means both "remedy" and "poison". So, during COVID, in the middle of a data desert, many governments, influenced by various interests espousing sometimes conflicting theories, decided to make medical choices for us, or at least those it could influence or force into compliance. As a result, the planet's general population became an experimental data sample. Sooner or later, a suitable sample size with more definitive results may appear. The data in mid-2025 appeared barely conclusive in terms of a rate of efficacy. It remains all about the data, *but not about all the data.*

The Daycroft Factor had compelled me to revisit both my Daycroft education, and the Plant and Animal Science courses I had studied at Rutgers more than 50 years prior to the Covid-19 pandemic. Also informative was my son's earlier response to my concern when his Marine Corps unit had been called up during the Iraq war, requiring him to be vaccinated against everything, including anthrax. His response to my concern when I expressed it to him: "Dad, if it doesn't hurt me, and it helps the Corps' mission, I'm good with it".

It was also quite clear that if I didn't get the two recommended COVID-19 vaccinations, I would not be getting on an airplane, going to a restaurant or other shared commercial space, or partake of any of the other things I had worked so hard to enjoy. With that and other information, and relying on intuition and reason grounded by The Daycroft Factor, I made a choice in June of 2020, unfettered by human hypothesis, and authorized by a power much higher than my own.

Hesitating, with conflicting public reports beginning to swirl, I had subsequently attempted to make an appointment in September for a Covid booster shot, which has since become referred to in our family as "the rooster booster". With lines for shots at the local CVS much longer than I chose to tolerate, and after spending hours on the phone one day trying to navigate the appointment process, I put the phone on speaker mode as my wife was preparing dinner that evening, so she could participate, opting to call an 800-number I was given after lashing out in frustration that day at someone else on the phone. My wife sometimes has a calming influence on me.

The woman who answered, whose accent I guessed was Philippine English, immediately asked who had given me the number. Before responding "the lady at CVS", I thought I heard a rooster crowing in the background. My request for her location was answered by "company policy prohibits me from providing that information". Company policy *did*, however, require her reading a lengthy legal disclaimer. Waiting patiently as the agent read the long disclaimer, I heard the rooster again, *twice,* the second more distinct than the first. I interrupted the disclaimer reading, and asked, "is that a rooster"? She affirmed, and continued. Moments later, as the disclaimer droned on, I heard the mother of all "cock-a-doodle- doo" noise a rooster could make. The woman on the other side of the world apologized, adding "he's at the screen door now". Eye contact with my wife surrendered both of us to convulsive laughter, after which a booster appointment was made at CVS.

A few days before that appointment, I had a slight cold and called our family physician to advise whether or not I should postpone. The response with which his nurse Elaine called me back was "Doctor wants you at *200 percent* if you get that booster. For some 30 years, I had often joked that our very data-driven noble physician might order a CT scan for a hangnail. So his recommendation, coming as it did amid news reports of adverse reactions from the boosters, was to me code for "no boosters, please". Recent data released in 2025 is beginning to suggest I made the right decision.

CHAPTER 3

Transitions

The Daycroft Middle School, 7th and 8th grades, provided a classic educational transition from the very nurturing elementary school experience, toward the final four years of a college preparatory education. Hormonal changes effecting human sexuality development, competitive tendencies, glimpses into adulthood, and related aspects of adolescence all converged with the goal of academic excellence at the Daycroft Middle School. This was not unlike many public educational environments at the time, with one major difference: the diligent effort to intersperse the ethics and morals of Christian Science throughout a student's entire experience continued to permeate each and every aspect of Daycroft's pedagogy and culture. A half century later, I came to recognize its profound possibilities for reversing the moral rot infecting a world so desperately in need of reform, including in, but not limited to, the world of education.

Each morning at the Daycroft School, children in grades 7 through 12 attended an assembly held in the large formal dining room of Adelaide Hall. Here, announcements of current and upcoming events, academic and athletic accomplishments, and other updates were made. Not infrequently, stern admonishments regarding scholarship by the erudite and personable Headmaster Joshua Lunt Smith were given to an assembly of about 150 students. A favorite exclamatory punctuation he often hurled at students, after outlining some needed academic or comportment adjustment was, "A word to the wise ... and the otherwise!". While The Daycroft School was not a parochial school per se, the influence of Mary Baker Eddy's Christian Science was obvious in his exhortations. A graduate of Bates College, holding also a Master's degree from Columbia, Joshua Lunt Smith had counseled me individually several times about the importance of confidence in working hard for scholarly attainment. His inscription to me in the 1962 Daycroft yearbook reads: "To Bruce - With great expectations from a Daycrofter! J.L.S. "

In keeping with Sara Pyle Smart's vison of both education and the doctrine of Christian Science as she understood it, each morning students heard the inspired words of the Bible, and thoughtful corroborations from the writings of Mary Baker Eddy. These readings were chosen and presented each day by different High School students. During my years at Daycroft, a few moments of silent prayer, followed by the audible repetition of the Lord's prayer in unison, was a daily recitation; and a hymn was sung, sometimes accompanied by musically talented students, but mostly by one remarkable music teacher, Mrs. Mary Brown. While some of the music was challenging for young pianists, children were encouraged to step up their chorale game by singing together as a unified student body during each morning's assembly, with members of the school's chorus providing leadership. The school's chorus was well respected in the Stamford, Connecticut community and surrounding area, its performances at Christmas sometimes broadcast by local radio stations, with recordings offered for sale to parents and friends of the school. The school's administration rarely missed an opportunity to integrate moral, ethical and spiritual precepts into Daycroft's curriculum and activities; the music of the Christian Science Church, rich in hymnary, was uplifting and often salutary in its depth of meaning, with students encouraged to correlate hymns with scriptural readings. Those who attended Daycroft from a very early age regarded it as a perfectly normal way to start the day.

In addition to its encouragement of good behavior and discipline - and to preclude wardrobe competitions among students, Daycroft students were required to wear a uniform. Beginning in 2nd grade, it consisted of a navy-blue blazer and long-sleeved blouse for both boys and girls, grey flannel or gabardine trousers for boys, grey skirts of similar material for girls; footwear consisted of Oxfords or loafers for boys, and saddle shoes or loafers for girls; high school girls lobbied for nylon hosiery and flats, which were officially adopted into the senior-year girls' uniform.

Behavioral standards were monitored daily, using the written point-based comportment/deportment system referenced earlier. Faculty members deducted points if they witnessed behavior which deviated from the very high moral and ethical standards students were being taught, and to which they were expected to adhere. But points were *not* awarded for excellent, exemplary behavior, because that was *expected* as a matter of course. Nothing bad happened for those who found themselves marked "A' or "B" or "C' groups, although the warning was clear below "A". "D" and "E" groups meant trouble, and loss of certain privileges. "E" group could also carry an additional delineation by the color red. If you were in "RED E" group, you were on thin ice, with expulsion from school a stated possibility, depending on the number and nature of transgressions involved.

Every polite nicety, from courtesy and coherent sentences to good table manners were encouraged by this system, supporting the occasional immediate, unhesitating reprimand by a faculty member who might witness something truly objectionable. Foul language put you straight into "E" group. The word "fuck", so coarsely and commonly a part of language among many of the young (and older) today, was never heard during school hours, nor were the facts of life it crudely referenced taught as part of the school's curriculum,

which included no basic biology, sex education, nor health courses
Nature still found a way. The windows of The Daycroft School bus
usually fogged up on the rides back from occasional evening visits
to New York's Metropolitan Opera or other cultural attractions.
These outings allowed pretty young girls to dress up and transform
themselves into beautiful young women, and requiring suits and ties
and shined shoes for boys. Kissing and adolescent groping, what was
termed at the time "making out" prevailed, as teen-age girls and boys
discovered without formal instruction the sweet natural tendencies
which defined their sexualities. Because of cost constraints, only
two faculty chaperones, generally younger teachers, would usually
accompany these cultural event field trips, usually taking two reserved
seats up front, to allow accurate head counts as students found their
seats toward the rear of the bus. At one point during a freezing
February Friday evening visit to the Metropolitan Opera in New York
City, having turned around to glance at his charges, a young male
teacher loudly exclaimed to his female counterpart "they're making
out like crazy back there!". She simply smiled and quietly commented
something to him. It was later circulated among the girl's dormitory
that she had said "It's a cold night; they're just staying warm". She
was well liked among middle school and high school students.

It was also during the Middle School and High School years during
the 1950s and early 1960s when many students began to more clearly
recognize the defining differences between The Daycroft School and
the rest of their world. Many students' parents were acutely aware of
the more progressive curricula and liberal influences to which their
children were being subtly exposed and by which they were being
indoctrinated while attending public schools in many areas, and they
wanted none of it. At the same time, divorce was becoming more
prevalent in post-WWII America, especially among wealthier couples,
for whom the loving, nurturing environment which Christian Science
offered their children was undoubtedly a major draw. By comparison
at that time, other religions, including notably the Roman Catholic
religion, with its doctrinal definition of marriage as a Sacrament,

and its prohibition of divorce, perhaps inadvertently stigmatized children whose parents' marriages were involved in various stages of dissolution. The Daycroft School became very much a family to such children. Among students whose homes were impacted by divorce were several from the homes of extremely wealthy and high-profile parents, including the The Getty and Revson (Revlon) families. It was also in the middle-school years when students not raised by wealthy parents became more aware of the differences in financial circumstances among parents. This, coupled with smaller class sizes, produced a status consciousness more pronounced than a student might find in the public schools, where kids could easily get lost in the crowd. Moral failings such as snobbishness, false pride, jealousy and resentment began to subtly undermine the fairly lofty moral and ethical standards which Daycroft's faculty worked to instill at every stage of student development.

In so many ways, for both middle-schoolers and High School students alike, my Daycroft experience of the 1950s and early 1960s reflected shifts in American culture which were generally prevalent in that era. Elvis Presley, Buddy Holly, Richet Valens, Jerry Lee Lewis, Fats Domino, The Everly Brothers, Carl Perkins, The Big Bopper and many other popular musicians too numerous to list but equally influential, reportedly competed for acceptance in a post-war baby-boomer youth culture that was more than willing to accept them. The Daycroft student population was no exception. By 1963, The Beatles and the "British Invasion" cultural phenomenon they inspired had consolidated the business and influences of popular music noticeably. The 1950s had been a simpler time, perhaps, but popular music still presented emotional reaction within the hearts and souls of pubescent boys and girls, as it likely always had. The intoxicating influence of popular music which teases - even glorifies - their budding sexuality was part of a popular culture which the Daycroft School faculty taught students to regard with spiritual discernment, if not outright disdain. Part of the reason for this was tied directly to the way in which the highly metaphysical aspects of the Christian Science lifestyle were perceived, supported, and represented by adults trying to practice it at Daycroft.

The emphasis on spiritual development of Daycroft students usually resulted in a puritanical view of human sexuality: generic man in absolute Christian Science was defined as spiritual, not material; therefore, anything which emphasized physicality, including sexual sensuality, was regarded as belonging to the lower elements of human consciousness and ontology. In the realm of the relative sense of things, Daycroft boys were instructed to contain "their animality". That instruction as communicated to Daycroft girls was reportedly more specific, designed to inspire virtues such as modesty, chastity, and feminine wisdom.

Indeed, nowhere was the divide between the Absolute and Relative sense of things more pronounced than within the area of human sexuality for teenagers at Daycroft. Abstention from vaguely unspecified sexual activity for adolescents often went unspoken, but came to be understood as the *only* acceptable form not only of self-control, but of birth control. There was no capitulation to the lust of the flesh, no psycho-babble regarding repressed sexuality, few tolerant accommodations of the age-old natural inquisitiveness and adventurousness of adolescent girls and boys. Unlike public school curricula, knowledge about sex and reproduction was not part of a biology or health course, as no such courses were offered at Daycroft. Such knowledge was usually gained in furtive, clandestine, sometimes hilarious conversations among students, in the back or front seats of cars, or in some secluded place. It was almost as if the subject among the faculty didn't exist. A memorable exception: during one post-practice pep talk the day before the first football game of a season, red faces and stifled guffaws resulted among team members when the coach instructed players who were between the ages of 14 and 18… "don't play with yourselves at night". He didn't say anything about sneaking off to rendezvous with nubile young girls willing to risk and endure the shame of being called a slut or worse, or of becoming pregnant, in order to do what biological nature has programmed the young to do throughout history.

In many ways, this standard helped students at Daycroft to focus on important spiritual, academic, athletic, and vocational training pursuits, undistracted to the extent possible by the sexual poison insinuated to be associated with the lower classes. Somehow, you were seen as holier and "better than" others if you rose above the physical attractions youngsters in any human culture normally have to each other. Catholic and other parochial schools were subject to these as well, but many approached the issue from a different, perhaps more practical standpoint, using fear of punishment and intimidation, rather than outright avoidance, as a method of choice.

The environment of the Middle School was extremely effective, however, in preparing students for the college preparatory work at which they would be expected to excel in High School. Notably, the encouragement to think critically, to question without fear of suppression, to stand up to bullies, to resist sloth and various temptations, and to strive for a higher and more complete understanding of things, including the universe, were developed in the very comprehensive pedagogy of the Daycroft Middle School. Events such as an impromptu Saturday night astronomy class, occasioned by the celestial clarity of a clear cold Connecticut January sky, featuring a bonfire, doughnuts, hot chocolate and cider provided ample opportunity for students to socialize, learn and yearn.

CHAPTER 4

Adolescence

A few weeks prior to the beginning of school in my eighth-grade year, a letter arrived at my parents' home. They had forwarded the letter to me at Crystal Lake Camps, the sleep-away summer camp to which they had, at great financial sacrifice, sent my sister and me most summers throughout my childhood. In very cordial wording, well written by the Senior Captain of the Varsity football team, Steve Harris, it offered a birth on the Junior Varsity football team, an invitation to try-out pre-season for a spot on the team. Thrilled and excited by this relatively formal outreach, the offer represented my first adolescent awareness of social construct and contract, and it was distinctly representative of The Daycroft Factor. The letter contained no vague mention of welcome, there was no hit-or-miss boilerplate general announcement in this invitation; no, this was a specific written invitation to a rite of passage. It spoke of older players' and coaches' observations of my abilities, enthusiasm and passion for athletics, and valued my place as a student at the school. *It made me feel good about myself, while at the same time insisting on my responsibilities to a school team.* Importantly, it came from a highly admired fellow student older than I, not a faculty member, although the Athletic Director/Coach was copied on the written communication.

What was not immediately apparent to me in the approach was that there were barely enough athletically-inclined students in the entire school to field both a soccer team and a football team at the same time in the Fall, and that the coaching staff was very small - as in one coach necessarily assigned to several different sports throughout the year, with well-intentioned but often unqualified faculty members assisting. A student team manager, usually of limited athletic potential or abilities, was assigned to administer much of the important detail management work, from preparing a portable blackboard and easel for the coach, to making sure equipment (much of it second-hand) was clean and in working order. Still, the invitation to participate was a milestone, representing a continuation of the transition already begun which is usually regarded as occurring somewhere between a child's 11th and 18tth year within the American educational system. As is the case today, an adolescent boys' period of development was as varied as it was formative.

My first distinct awareness of sexuality generally, and of my own specifically, had revealed itself only a couple of years prior. It was during that period that I discovered my intensely delightful feelings of yearning toward members of the opposite sex. The first partner in my growing fascination was a beautiful early bloomer Daycrofter, Judy Vetter. Judy was crowned with long brunette hair, dark shining eyes, and a smile that could stop a clock. We kissed on the lips at Hubbard Heights Park in Stamford, Connecticut when I was 12 years old. What a magical feeling: Touching! Feeling! Arousal! Distraction! Frustration! Motivation! They all seemed to coalesce in a merry mesmeric mush of awareness and enchantment. Attractive female teachers and other fully mature pretty ladies in my sphere of acquaintance even became seen through the lens of increasingly apparent sexuality. These feelings were increasingly accompanied or followed by an undefined sense of guilt and embarrassment, conflicting as they did with the lofty metaphysical values taught at Daycroft. This conflict remained during the teenage years to come. Homework, independent study, mandatory study halls for boarding students, unannounced "pop" quizzes in class, field trips to Ivy League College campuses and sporting events, participation in various academic honor societies, Student Council, chorus, art classes, field trips to New York City an hour away, were all a major part of increased exposure to cultural development during Middle School, and later at the Preparatory School. It was during this period that I began to understand the beauty of knowledge, the clarity of well-formed thoughts, words, and sentences, the intellectual provability of mathematics – all balanced by the physical release of athletics, sports, and youthful romance. It was an intoxicating transition from being nurtured by those assigned to instruct and guide, to learning the adult value of being instructed, nurtured, and guided by oneself toward one's positive self-interest. The Middle School years were indeed transitional and transformative. They were, in some ways, the most formative of my entire childhood.

One of the attributes often referred to by faculty – courage and zeal tempered by wisdom - was once demonstrated by a fellow student, Jeff Squires, an eighth grader of above average height, weight, and intelligence, who had taken to weight-lifting in preparation for playing football and other sports. My parents having moved to Stamford to be closer to the school, we travelled on the same school bus each day. One afternoon, an older, powerfully built Daycroft football player, whose prowess on the gridiron had earned him honorable mention at the League level, decided to taunt and bully the younger athlete as the bus was being boarded, going so far as to slap him in the face during the banter while he was seated. The younger boy stood up with trepidation ready to respond with a punch; but aware of a host of adverse consequences for himself, for the older student, and for the school, this eighth grader jutted out his jaw, looked the older student squarely in the eye, and stared him down. By this time, other students were rallying to the younger boy's cause, urging the bully to leave him alone. The peer pressure worked: seeing the reaction of other schoolmates, the bully backed off with a warning to the eighth grader to watch his back, and returned to his seat on the bus. Jeff was never bullied by him again.

Sexual boundaries were also best taught by fellow students. In addition to housing the school library, its main kitchen, dining facilities, a few classrooms, and the girl's dormitory, Adelaide Hall sat atop a cavernous finished basement, where art classes were taught, table-tennis and shuffleboard could be played, and weekend social events were sometimes held. It also served as one of several civil defense facilities at the school. One day during the lunch break, a very pretty, vivacious coquette of perhaps 13 years and I had ventured into a dimly lit area to explore an absolutely delightful activity. With hearts pounding from the mystery of erotic desire spurred by adolescent groping, we heard an adult calling out at the top of the stairs that the dining room was ready to close, and that those who hadn't taken lunch yet should do so at that time. We both recognized the improbability that this teacher was making a general announcement. Not wanting to miss lunch, we began to climb the stairs together, and I gently placed my hand on the coquette's derriere. Giving me a demurring smile, her beautiful eyes speaking volumes, she firmly removed my hand with a clear indication that she would not tolerate nor risk being seen allowing such a public display of affection. Months later on a cold February night during a return bus ride back from a school-sponsored visit to New York's Metropolitan Opera, things escalated. As she sat on my lap under the cover of dark, she allowed me to explore her thighs, at the last minute sweetly making it gaspingly clear that she enforced boundaries as to how far I would be allowed to go with her. It was in this way that I and others learned to respect, if not fully understand, the wishes of the opposite sex, and to control our animality, while being rendered utterly and completely hypnotized by this delightfully enchanting thing called sex. There was no sense of rejection or resentment involved, simply a resolution based on respect, driven by the female of the species, and artfully reinforced by Daycroft's Faculty and administration.

CHAPTER 5

Athletics: Distinguishing Between the Absolute and the Relative in the Physical World

From simple concepts to complex, noble intentions attended the interactions of spirituality and materiality at Daycroft. Beginning in early adolescence, students increasingly learned to understand growth in all aspects of human development, including intellectual stimulation, the challenges of competitive sports, intelligent discourse, character development, and in the transition occurring toward adulthood. Everything was being influenced and supported by the ethics and morals of Christian Science.

My high school freshman year at Daycroft extended the transition from boyhood to manhood. Differences between things of the Spirit, and things of the flesh, intimated during earlier childhood formation, were more clearly revealed during my entry into competitive scholastic sports. These revelations both diminished my childish hero worship of older student athletes, replaced by an instinctive desire to compete, while at the same time venerating great athletes in general. In the process, I began to learn the rugged succession of commitments, sacrifices, toils and risks which accompanied competitive team sports. The lessons learned in competitive interscholastic team contests, and the memories of achievements through participation in them, have often provided moments of reflection and clarity throughout my life.

Daycroft athletes were expected to "Perceive then Demonstrate" the very high moral and ethical standards of Christian Science in both team cooperation and interscholastic competition. Competing primarily against other private schools allowed Daycrofters to do so with athletes of varied backgrounds, often with dramatically unpredictable results. Once, toward the end of a football game against what was known in the league at the time as "a rich-kids reform school", Cedar Knolls, Daycroft was leading by two touchdowns, when a Cedar Knolls defensive back initiated an intentional vicious late tackle, out of bounds, against Stu Carlough, a strong Daycroft running back who had scored earlier in the game. As the referee threw his penalty flag, Stu tossed off his helmet and menaced the offender, who wisely chose not to engage; instead, the players from the opposing school decided their losing was the fault of the referee, whom they proceeded to assault on the field. Both benches and some students emptied onto the field as a melee ensued; the referee immediately forfeiting the game to Daycroft. As team co-Captain, I and several other teammates escorted the referee safely to his car. Faculty from both schools were soon able to restore order, positioning themselves between very angry Daycroft players and sore losers from Cedar Knolls itching for a rumble.

Another fracas involved a lanky Daycroft basketball player, Steve Heubeck. After being intentionally tripped during a game, ironically by a player from Cedar Knolls - Steve, who subsequently served as a paratrooper in the United States Army after college, and later had a distinguished career as a commended FBI Special Agent, happened to be an accomplished martial artist as a teenager. He also conceived translating the Daycroft School Motto "Perceive then Demonstrate" to Latin, which appeared on the cover of the 1961 yearbook, The Milestone, when he was on its student staff. After being tripped while driving for a lay-up in a basketball game, he quickly bounced up off the floor fully prepared to exact punishment for the foul; however, both his martial arts training and The Daycroft Factor had taught Steve discipline under such circumstances, even as the tripper taunted him. The offending player was ejected, free-throws were made, and Steve was praised for his self-control – a coachable moment from which we all learned. It should be noted however that to let him cool off, the coach sat Steve out for the next few minutes of the game, which Daycroft won.

Numerous other episodic tests of sportsmanship, discipline and discretion occurred regularly throughout my sports activities at Daycroft. Once during a basketball game at Hamden Hall, an opponent grabbed my jersey from behind as I was trying to position myself for a play. Irritated, I cursed at him loudly while throwing an elbow to his gut, which unintentionally got the attention of the referee, causing him to see only my elbow to the opponent's gut, and my rival's feigning innocence. He was awarded two foul shots, both of which he sunk. I was charged with the foul, and was benched. My coach's subsequent instruction to me after the game was clear and correct: "never retaliate on the court or field during a game – because the ref may or may not see your opponent's foul, but *will invariably* see your retaliation; referees will only call what they see".

Such episodes were part and parcel of the numerous coachable moments rarely missed by the school's long-time athletic director, a most influential figure at Daycroft, Coach Bill Fisher. A math teacher as well as serving as Athletic Director and varsity coach, Coach Fisher had completed his teaching degree requirements at nearby Bridgeport University while on the faculty of Daycroft. He, his wife, and two daughters resided in a lovely cottage on the far side of the playing fields, away from the dormitories and academic class buildings, but near the gymnasium. A rugged and resourceful man, Bill Fisher had reportedly been a cowboy at one point in his early adulthood. Coaching several sports at Daycroft, Coach Fisher's decidedly masculine influence was sometimes at odds with an environment in which gentility and cultural refinement were highly valued. He was known to vigorously object when a very attractive dance teacher, Mia Paul, would schedule late afternoon ballroom dance and cotillion classes, which conflicted with football practice in the days before a big game. A diligent teacher of fundamentals during practices, Coach Fisher made clear his objectives from the sidelines on game day, sometimes impatiently, but always with the objective of teaching, and winning games.

While Coach Fisher knew how to tape ankles, and encouraged during practices the physical fitness required to play interscholastic football at the high school level, the two areas in which he was somewhat deficient were in sports physiology and sports medicine. This may have been a deficiency resulting from misunderstandings surrounding Christian Science, and its manifest attitudes toward modern medicine at that time, and since. In fairness, modern sports medicine as it had developed over the next 60 years was in its infancy when this good man coached varsity sports. Concussions, sprains, and other injuries often went undiagnosed or misdiagnosed, with medical treatment, if sought, pushed off-campus. Once, a very talented teammate, who had transferred to Daycroft from Saint Paul's School in Long Island, suffered a painful shoulder injury, possibly a rotator cuff tear. A few weeks later, his very pretty girlfriend, Gail Reed, confided to me that Coach Fisher, his good intentions perhaps overshadowed by missing a key player's prowess on the gridiron, had asked him good-naturedly, "What kind of Christian Scientist are you?".

The metaphysics involved in Christian Science healing declare man, in Absolute terms, made in God's image and likeness, to be perfect – upright, whole, and free. This perception has been associated with cases of physical healing. However, the mere tool of human language generally describes things in Relative terms, as in "torn rotator cuff".

The difference between The Absolute and the Relative is one clearly made by one of Mrs. Eddy's early students, judge Septimus Hanna, who in fact wrote an article entitled The Absolute and the Relative, which was published in The Christian Science Journal a year after Mrs. Eddy's passing. It appears to have been confined to the Archives of The Mother Church, The First Church of Christ, Scientist, in Boston for many decades, and likely not an essay with which most Daycroft School faculty members were familiar.

My own first-hand awareness of the Daycroft School's deficiencies in dealing with physical injuries had occurred when my ring finger was badly dislocated while playing in my next-to-last football game in my junior year. After holding my hand up while indicating I needed to come off the field, I was instructed to sit on the bench. While likely in a state of minor traumatic shock holding my left hand, nauseated by the sight on the distal portion of my ring finger at right angles to the rest, trying to avoid looking at it, I became aware of a stranger, not affiliated with the school, approaching me; without saying much, he took my hand and jerked the finger back into place. He then taped it to the two adjacent fingers, and disappeared. Speculation later arose as to who the stranger was – a scout from a rival team? A professional player who had just happened to be there, knew what to do, and had done it before? An athletic trainer from the opponent team's school, perhaps? Whomever he was, in a very brief moment of intense pain, the finger was snapped back into place, and eventually healed. A few years earlier, my father had sacrificed to buy a piano and provide me with classical lessons from a concert pianist who played regularly at Carnegie Hall and lived in nearby Cos Cob, Elizabeth Hipple Yates. While he forbade me from playing in the final game of the season, or even attend practice, no one on the school's staff

ever inquired about, nor even mentioned the injury in my presence.
I found this curious, but accepted it as normal.

That painful episode paled in comparison to the major injury I
suffered in my Senior year at Daycroft. It happened during the first
play from scrimmage following our kick-off, in a Friday afternoon
game at The Roosevelt School near Shippan Point in Stamford.
Like the majority of seniors who played both offense and defense,
the defensive captain and I, with just one word – decided what had
to be done - sack Roosevelt's quarterback to get things started. After
busting through their line and bearing down on him, he nimbly
and quickly scrambled sharply to his right, and as I tried to change
direction, my aluminum cleats dug deep into the Connecticut turf,
and disaster struck: every connective tissue in my left knee was torn
asunder within the seconds that followed. In agony, I was helped
off the field by teammates, instructed by Coach to sit on the bench,
and told to let him know when I was ready to return to the game. I
would not be ready for the rest of the season, as it was later diagnosed
as a major tear of meniscus cartilage, tendons and ligaments. After
the game, my girlfriend, recognizing the noticeable swelling, and
that I could not put any weight on the leg, helped me to her car, and
drove me to Stamford hospital. My parents could not immediately be
reached, so I called my sister Ellie, who lived in Stamford. Later that
evening, her husband, Ed Czyr, collected me from the hospital and
brought me to their home, where I spent a very painful, traumatic,
sleepless night on a couch in their living room. My father arrived
at 6:00 am Saturday morning to take me home, producing a pair
of crutches later that afternoon. I could not put any weight on my
left leg, which was badly swollen at the knee, and I was in a lot of
pain. My mother called a Christian Science Practitioner friend,
who offered me words of comfort and prayer, in what was known in
Christian Science parlance as "a treatment". On Monday afternoon,
my dad, a pragmatic and well-educated man, clandestinely took
me to a renowned orthopedic surgeon affiliated with New York's
Columbia Presbyterian Hospital, who examined me and diagnosed

torn meniscus cartilage, and a major tear of anterior and probably posterior cruciate ligaments.

At the time, exploratory open-knee surgery, possibly involving removal of part or all of the cartilage, and visual inspection and treatment of the ligament damage, if possible, was the only surgical remedy immediately available. The good Doctor informed me and my father that good results were not guaranteed, and he recommended against the surgery. He prescribed instead a physical therapy rehabilitation protocol involving heat/cold therapy, weight training to build muscle and prevent atrophy of the leg muscles, and the gradual re-introduction of mobility without the aid of crutches.

Because I was unable to drive a car with its manual clutch transmission foot pedal, my parents were able to negotiate a small room at the new Daycroft School Greenwich campus. Navigating the stairs while on crutches was quite difficult, and I was generally miserable with the situation. My girlfriend, with whom I had been keeping company and had fallen in love over the previous year, prevailed upon her parents to offer that I could live with them for a while, so that she could drive us in her car to school each day until things improved; it was an offer my Dad reluctantly accepted, despite the strong disapproval of my mother, who was not a fan of my relationship with this young woman. My mother had even gone so far as to put a lock on the rotary dialer common to telephones at that time, to prevent my calling her. Our young love found a way: during the school day, she would let me know approximately what time she would be calling that evening, letting the phone ring twice; it was my signal to call her from a phone booth nearby. This and related efforts on my mother's part to discourage the relationship caused enormous resentment and confusion on my part, and a deterioration of my relationship with both my parents, at an age and under circumstances when emotions ran high under the best of circumstances.

As the recovery capabilities of a healthy 17-year-old enabled me to walk without assistance, the knee stabilized over the next few months, and grew stronger with the physical therapy regimen I tried to follow. Unbeknownst to me at the time, an involuntary behavior modification was developing, as I unconsciously favored my left leg. My right leg being my dominant leg, the behavior modification went unnoticed. Happily, limited participation in basketball was possible, which I enjoyed that winter. However, the knee damage was a source of repeated injury in college, ending my football aspirations, continuing to be a painful re-injury reminder well into my twenties and early thirties during recreational sports activities. Surgery remained an unacceptable risk. However, I was grateful to be able to resume sports such as skiing and running, and even officiated soccer games some 20 years later, but always consciously and perhaps subconsciously favoring the left leg. The conflict within my own consciousness between the things of Spirit, and the things of the flesh, between the Absolute and the Relative, remained a conundrum. My return to studying the writings of Mary Baker Eddy, and some of her early students, combined with explosive growth in "health clubs" amid the resurgent emphasis on physical fitness throughout the 1970s, 1980s, and 1990s, encouraged me to revisit the fundamentals learned at Daycroft, and were indeed restorative to my health. In 1974, I actually began attending church services at a Christian Science church near my home, which, unbeknown to me at the time, was brewing a major controversy in that denomination, which would eventually be settled through litigation by the New Jersey State Supreme Court. The church was located on Prospect Avenue in Plainfield, New Jersey, not far from the home in Edison my wife and I had established early in our marriage.

There were three other coaches at Daycroft whose tenures at the school were quite salutary. One was a 6'7" UCLA graduate, Scott Fitzrandolph, who played and coached basketball well. He immediately recognized and built a team around the exceptional talent of a blonde-haired, blue eyed Sophomore lad from Brooklyn NY, Bob Luongo. "Bongo" spent his summers playing pick-up games on the outdoor courts of Adelphi Academy and other locations in New York

City, with players who had neither blonde hair nor blue eyes, and regarded the game as a potential ticket out of city poverty. Another very tall player, the late Bert Peterson, added a powerful rebounding and scoring talent to the team; Coach Fitzrandolph balanced Bongo's exceptional shooting and passing talents with the developmental needs of the other players, made playing basketball enjoyable, and coached winning seasons despite a rather shallow bench of players. Bob Luongo was the leader on the court, frequently signaling others as to what to do next, making any coach's job much easier.

The school's Junior Varsity football coach was a red-haired Dutchman named Janssen, a 1951 graduate of Principia College. He also taught science, and occasionally doubled as a soccer coach for the school's fledgling soccer team. During Junior Varsity football practice sessions, he would sometimes chastise eighth and ninth graders with a smiling, good-natured, but effective "you're like vanilla pudding, guys! Anticipate, hit hard, push him where you want him to go!" If a player didn't do that in practice, he would, with a smile, just say … "vanilla pudding". During the late August heat of pre-season training, his weight-loss encouragement consisted his good-natured singing of the title from a popular 1942 Jazz and Pop song, recorded by Glenn Miller in 1944: "It must be jelly, 'cause jam doesn't shake like that"! While he often punctuated his coaching with laughter, he was hard as nails, with character and leadership skills nonpareil, and was an inspiration for the school's students of all ages. Once, during a Junior Varsity game against a very strong Fairfield private school, a Daycroft player, Robert Mahler, was tackled hard, leaving him writhing in pain on the field. The coach and trainer from the other school ran out to assist, but Mr. Janssen growled them away, with accusations that their pretending to care was an act, an ill- concealed attempt to cover up their desire to run up the score. They backed off quickly.

Another great coach was a former Columbia University coach, Verne Ullom, who was married to a teacher at the Daycroft School, and served as chaperone/director of the Boy's Dormitory located in the upper floors of Hill House. He took a special liking to my interest in tennis, and coached me in the sport in my sophomore year, after it became clear that my eyesight made my hitting a pitched baseball, except by chance, unlikely. He took it upon himself to see to it that I played varsity interscholastic tennis in the Spring of my Sophomore and Junior years. A large, muscular man, having grown children of his own, he knew how to handle adolescent boys and commanded their respect without having to intimidate them. He once extracted a splinter from the sole of my foot, which had lodged there during horseplay while barefoot on wooden floors in Hill House, which were probably due for a sanding. "Sit still!" he growled as his massive hands removed the splinter with needle and razor blade, cleansing the wound site with disinfectant, and applying a band-aide. "Wear shoes up here next time" he pointedly and gruffly advised, "In fact, your parents paid for you to have shoes, so wear them," adding with a grin, "unless you're swimming". He then added, "Honor thy father and thy mother", turned, and walked out of the room.

Mr. Ullom's inscription to me in the 1962 Milestone, Daycroft's yearbook, reads as follows:

"To Daycroft's version of the Australian 'Laurie' game: The sophistication of an athlete is only superficial. It's the inner realization of one's real source of strength, courage, and desire that enables a student of Christian Science to 'work, work, work, watch and pray'. It has been a pleasure to know and coach you. Mr. and Mrs. Ullom."

I have often remembered with great fondness, respect and inspiration Coach Ullom's tireless encouragement of my tennis game in the Spring of 1962. I later learned that his Milestone Yearbook message to me was a quote from Mary Baker Eddy, the inspired thinker of the 19th century, whose 19th century ministry established the Christian Science movement. If not for that inscription, I would never have known of his clearly deep interest in things of the Spirit, versus the things of the flesh.

So very often, the important lessons learned in athletic activities from my earliest years at Daycroft have provided transport across the divide all too apparent to the corporeal senses, between the Absolute and the Relative sense of things, between the Spirit and the flesh.

CHAPTER 6

Glorious Summers in the Allegheny Mountains

Until the summer of 1962, I spent as many summers as my parents could struggle to afford at Crystal Lake Camps, high in the Allegheny Mountains of North Central Pennsylvania. It, too, was owned and operated by Christian Scientists; and my parents' sacrifice to send me there was something I learned to truly appreciate years later, both as a parent myself, and as a student of Christian Science.

Crystal Lake Camps was and remains a beautifully bucolic campus of about 1,000 acres, where children and staff from all over the world come each summer to enjoy and learn, in an atmosphere of generally tranquil ambiance. A fully accredited American Camp Association camp, most of the activities normally associated with a summer camp for children were offered: a Red Cross compliant swimming program, canoeing and small-craft sailing, mountain hiking, camping, horseback riding, including overnight camping trips on horseback, group and individual sports, archery, group games such as capture the flag, introduction to Native American culture, arts and crafts, and week-long canoe trips down the Susquehanna river. Families were also invited to visit during the off-season, to enjoy cross-country skiing and other winter activities. There was usually a very modest fee charged, which made such visits ideal for budget-conscious young families. Long winter weekend breaks offered cross-country skiing, ice skating, snow-shoeing, and hot chocolate in front of a roaring fire. A beautiful new octagonal dining hall, built in 1970, large and rustic, had a huge Pennsylvania stone fireplace, on which camp owner Dottie Alford was known to grill marinated venison steaks, often donated by hunters she would allow to hunt the property during deer season free of charge, in keeping with her keen understanding of the humane need to cull herds, precluding them from freezing or starving to death in bitter cold Allegheny Mountain winters. During an early Spring visit in 2003, she also served me chipped bear steak on toast for breakfast in a Bechamel sauce one morning. A friend who hunted during bear season in Maine had sent her the steaks, frozen and shrink-wrapped during that winter. It was quite delicious, and I realized as an adult the practical resourcefulness and unique quality of Dottie Alford's character.

There were numerous wild blueberry bushes in and around the camp. Campers of all ages would regularly harvest blueberries, driven by a friendly competition among cabins, with the younger campers' cabins given a sizeable bucket count handicap. The cabin judged to have harvested the most blueberries would enjoy an extra homemade blueberry pie for their table at supper. Somehow every cabin won at least once during the summer - even the youngest - with campers learning kindness from their big brother's and sister's wink and a nod at seeing the joy the younger campers experienced.

Other Daycroft students attended Crystal Lake Camps as well, so a sense of continuity and camaraderie was often present. So deep was the appreciation for summers at camp, that when I was cajoled in 2002 by Camp Owner Dottie Alford, a widow by then, to serve on its board of directors, I felt moved to agree. Serving on the camp's board was a truly cathartic experience, during which I spearheaded the legal effort to save the camp from a local scoundrel, a pernicious gadfly who was alleged to snooker those who owned property in the mountains, including camp owner Dottie Alford, into selling their properties to him. His intent was later alleged to be a nefarious attempt to profit from the sale of drilling and fracking lease rights in the shale-rich mountain on which this beautiful camp had operated for more than 60 years. The camp itself had later negotiated with several energy companies, to sell drilling and fracking rights in remote sections of the camp in the distant future.

It was at this camp where I learned, as a child, that there were many campers who were being raised in Christian Science, but who attended public schools in various parts of the United States and other countries. This helped to normalize the somewhat cloistered approach to my childhood formation which my parents sought to provide with a Daycroft education. Neighborhood children at home would sometimes taunt me about Christian Science, parroting their parents' ignorance of it in a mean-spirited way, which likely reflected their parents' approach to such things. Crystal Lake Camps during the summer allowed a respite from such peer pressure.

At the formative age of 10, I met a young man who would indelibly imprint his salutary countenance on my consciousness for the rest of my life. David Purdy, nicknamed "Waldo" by staff and campers, was everything a young adolescent boy could look up to, and be encouraged to emulate. An UCLA PhD candidate and United States Marine Corps Captain serving in the Reserves at the time, Waldo possessed the intelligence and wry sense of humor marking him as a leader in every aspect of his summer employment. A Bates College graduate from New England, Waldo taught the value and discipline of regular vigorous exercise, honesty, respect for the rights of others, a sense of humor, deep appreciation for the sanctity and beauty of nature, and the ever-present encouragement of campers to do their best at whatever they undertook. He had the uncanny ability to zero in on a boy's personality and talents, and bring out the best in him. My parents were older than most parents of a 10-year-old at that time. After speaking with them, and understanding the financial sacrifices they had made to provide both the summer camp and Daycroft School experiences, Waldo took me under his wing, and encouraged me daily, offering declarations such as "you're different" – a declaration which I initially misunderstood, and to which I regularly and vociferously objected. Over the course of one pre-pubescent summer, Waldo convinced me of what he meant, and taught me to be grateful, but not prideful, of this. Over the next few summers, as I entered adolescence, Waldo taught me what true leadership looked like; that most things of value required diligence and often hard work to achieve; that work should be done with gratitude for the ability, and a joyful willingness, to do it; that respect for others begins with respect for oneself; that one should never allow oneself to be intimidated by a bully, and how to deal with one; that being different sometimes meant being able to laugh at oneself without embarrassment.

Observing that my parents, hopeful of cultivating my love of music, had given me a bugle to bring to camp, Waldo assigned me at age 12 to bugle early-morning Reveille, for which I had no training, and limited lung capacity at that age. However, Waldo advised me to reach out to the music director to learn. Making more noise than music, I struggled through the early-morning assignments each day that summer, incurring good-natured teasing from other campers, which Waldo taught me to accept in the spirit in which it was usually intended, and to use it as a motivation to strive for mastery of the bugle. At one evening's daily flag-lowering ceremony, Waldo asked me to fill in for the councilor who normally performed bugle duties, playing the classic "Retreat" rendition for the flag-lowering ceremony. Extremely nervous, but willing to try, I absolutely butchered the performance, which produced uncontrollable guffaws and groans from both campers and counselors, but I muddled through. As was customary prior to flag-lowering, Waldo had calmly issued the order "retire the colors"; then, as the evening birds sang their praise that the bugle bungle was over, as the flag was being removed from the halyard, Waldo just as calmly, although pointedly in good nature, without casting his steel-blue eyes in my direction, ordered "retire the bugler", producing peals of laughter throughout the sizable gathering of campers and staff; from this I learned the humility to laugh at myself when what I did was embarrassing to me but unintentionally comical, and not to fear failure.

The Red Cross required that a person reach the age of 15 before being eligible for its Water Safety Aide certification. Waldo often encouraged my swimming abilities, and he often encouraged campers to develop leadership skills. In my case, he went out of his way to write a letter to the Red Cross, asking for an exception to the rule for me, which was granted. I was thus able to serve as an assistant on the Waterfront staff the following summer, as a Councilor in Training. After later completion of the complete Red Cross Water Safety Instructor certification at Rutgers a few years later, I was able to land a very lucrative Waterfront Director job at the exclusive Breezemont Day Camp in Armonk New York, within commuting distance from my parent's home. This enabled me to earn additional compensation transporting several campers who lived outside the camp bus route to and from camp each day. So handsome was the pay, that I was able to fund much of my tuition and living costs throughout the ensuing college school year.

Waldo was also acutely aware of the natural tendencies and temptations which his campers would soon face. Accompanying them to a nearby small County Fair one summer evening, I and several others were given a dollar or two, and allowed to wander off together, with orders to rendezvous at a specified time and designated location. Soon thereafter, transfixed by the sight of scantily clad dancers undulating on a stage while advertising ticket sales for a strip-tease performance in the adjoining tent, my pals and I felt the large hands of several councilors grabbing us by the scruff of our necks, and dragging us out from among the assembled gawkers. Waldo's chidings as we made our way back to the camp van were understanding and humorous, leaving no feelings of guilt or shame.

When I was 13, Waldo gave me a copy of The Red Cross Family Relations Guide for Men. It was the first and only actual sex education I ever had in book or educational form at any point of my young formation. More than anything else at that point of my development, it helped me understand and address as natural and normal the incessant sexual impulses which all adolescents face, and to respect women.

Waldo had become my best adult friend as well as my councilor. He helped me cross that bridge in life from childhood to adolescence, teaching me to joyfully approach the future with confidence, and a deep appreciation for goodness, the beauty of nature, and gratitude. In one conversation, he advised me to always strive to do my best at whatever I did, because one cannot, by definition, do better than one's best. He taught me at an early age to distinguish between an Absolute sense of things, and a relative one.

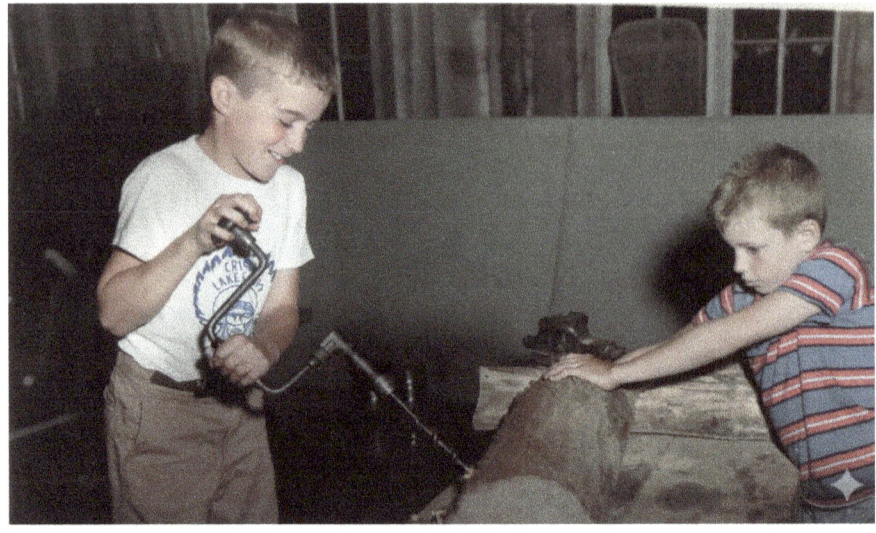

Camp closed each year after an eight-week season, but parents were encouraged to allow older campers to stay an extra week or so to help get the camp ready for the off-season. My parents were happy to offer my time for splitting firewood, readying canoes, floats, tennis nets and other camp equipment for storage, grooming and feeding the horses, and other chores designed to keep youngsters busy. Waldo was among those counselors paid to stay; during that week, he casually let me know the next stage of his life was approaching, that he would be finishing up his PhD work soon, and probably entering the foreign service or similar full-time work. In the days leading up to his departure back to California, I developed a sad, apprehensive foreboding that I might never see him again. On the day he was to fly back to California, I helped carry his heavy luggage the distance on the gravel road between Norman Lodge in the boy's camp and Laughlin Lodge near the camp entrance. It was a quiet walk, and his keen intuition must have informed him how I felt. After helping load his luggage into the station wagon that would take him to the airport, he gazed down at me, extended his hand for a handshake, and addressing me quietly by name, said "I don't believe in goodbyes; I want you to work hard and play hard throughout your life, and always do your best. We'll write each other, ok?" The sadness I felt was alleviated by a brief embrace, his driver mentioned what time his flight was scheduled, and he got into the passenger's side, flashed me a smile and a thumbs-up, and the crunching of tires on gravel signaled a tremendous sense of loss and a previously unknown need to grieve. There was a favorite footpath through the woods back to the boy's camp off the road; sobbing and wailing the distance back to Norman lodge, I experienced an overwhelming sense of loss and despair, unlike anything I had ever felt, collapsed onto my bunk, fell fast asleep, and awoke to see the moon against a clear Allegheny Mountain sky, before again visiting sleep's healing refuge.

Waldo's influence was missed after his professional life prevented his return to Camp. He kept in touch with campers over the winter while finishing his PhD, writing letters of encouragement, even sending me a 45 rpm copy of a popular Del Vikings' tune, "Come Go with Me", which Waldo had played at high volume on a record player each morning in the campers' cabin; he sent me William Danforth's classic, "I Dare You", which encourages confidence and courage among young people; and he later sent Henry Drummond's book "The Greatest Thing in the World", an inspirational book extolling the concept of Love as life's supreme virtue. Later in life, Waldo was a founder of the first college in the United States devoted exclusively to environmental studies – Unity College - in Unity Maine. Unity became a university in 2023, renamed Unity Environmental University. Alumni of Unity College were placed in environmental jobs in New England and throughout the United States in roles such as Park and Recreation department staff.

Generally undiscovered or perhaps overlooked at Crystal Lake Camps was that boyish camaraderie with campers in the girl's camp was increasingly less than wholesome, and sometimes dangerous. It included clandestine night time visits with teen-age girls across Crytal Lake, with nocturnal skinny-dips on the itinerary. The giggles and squeals of teenage girls for whose charms we were willing to risk being caught during these nocturnal aquatic missions were stifled sufficiently, in order to avoid detection. Ultimately, virtue prevailed, but oh, the thrill of anticipated kinesthetic tactile stimulation!

The hypnotic influence of adolescent sexuality lurked daily, particularly during the changeover at mealtimes, when the girls' camp was exiting the Long House dining hall to make room for their counterparts in the boy's camp. Supervised Saturday night socials, often featuring musical performances by camper musicians, provided an opportunity to actually physically embrace members of the opposite sex. Dancing to popular tunes played on a stereo fanned lustful aspiration among we 15-year-old boys, some of whom took to wearing athletic supporters to hide our inevitable signs of sexual arousal when dancing with young women. On Sunday afternoons, older campers and staff scheduled and enjoyed joint free swims in Crystal Lake, during which young women in bathing suits often produced palpable adolescent libido response from both boys and girls. This often recommended staying submerged from the neck down to hide an inevitable quite natural response. A young woman's nubile body in a one-piece bathing suit was known to send many a lad into a daze of enchantment.

Adolescent attraction to members of the opposite sex became stronger at about the time Counsellors-in-Training were beginning to question their own involvement in camping. Toward the end of the summer after Waldo had successfully defended for his PhD dissertation, the wheels began to fall off any tolerance or respect some of us had for adults' supervision of our sexuality. One afternoon during a free period, three of my pals and I thought it a terrific idea to produce an audio tape recording of our feelings, using a tape recorder one of us had brought to the camp. The gist of this stupidity was to crudely and explicitly suggest that camp Director Dottie Alford should keep her nose out of our sex lives. We finished our recording with smug pride and laughter, and went off to our activities.

A few nights later, the entire camp attended a traditional annual lakeside gathering of the tribes. This ceremony highlighted a lakeside Council Fire against a backdrop of authentic Indian Tee-Pees, erected with the help of local members of the Lenape tribe. The ceremony venerated native American culture, including native American dances and a moving address offered by Joe Alford, Dottie Alford's husband, who was dressed for the occasion in actual Native American regalia, including an authentic Chieftain's headdress. Much importance was attached to this ceremony, as it provided a summary of the blessings campers had enjoyed during the summer, and encouraged deep reflection by all campers and staff. The Council Fire was traditionally followed by a night of complete silence for both girls' and boys' camps ... an impressive undertaking only rarely interrupted by whispers, murmurs, and giggles.

During the Camp owner's homily a large muscular counselor, a popular Penn State wrestler nicknamed "Scotty", backed by an equally stalwart counselor nicknamed "Sam", approached me and each of my three clan leader friends. One by one, Scotty thrust a pointed finger into our chests, prodding us silently but unmistakenly to follow him away from the council fire, to a nearby panel truck. He told us to get in, and then drove us to our cabin, with no explanation but that we should maintain the silence befitting the sanctity of council fire night; "keep your mouths shut" did the trick. Once in the cabin, he instructed us to load our bunkbeds onto the truck, bedclothes included, and to hop up onto the back of the truck. We nervously wondered about our fate, but said nothing during the bumpy ride in the Allegheny Mountain darkness, pierced only by the old truck's head lights and the roar of its engine. When we arrived at the walk-out entrance to the basement of the camp owners' lakeside lodge, we were ordered to help each other carry our beds inside, and wait there, in silence. Shortly thereafter, the camp owner appeared in the doorway, carrying a tape recorder. We froze as he plugged it in and turned it on, adjusting the volume. Unnerved by the icy glare of Scotty, Sam, and the owner, we sat trembling and managed to stifle nervous laughter at the foul language we had <u>used</u>, looking down at the floor, lest by looking at each other our embarrassment would erupt into nervous laughter, and we would all surely be killed.

When those assembled had heard all of it, each of the adults made a clear and compelling statement of their disappointment in us, and disgust with what they had just heard. The camp owner, clearly angry, watched us squirm without saying a word. In turn, Scotty and Sam asked us if we had any objection to sharing the tape with our parents. One of our fathers was a Lt. General in the Army, another a Navy Captain. My own father had been a Canadian soldier and hockey player, who had a temper, and was known to have committed violence during his life against injustice. For an hour, we were berated and browbeaten for what we had done, and it was made clear that our character required reform. Then we learned our fate. We would be separated during the day for a week, each under the supervision of senior counselors, who would supervise our study of scriptures and the denominational textbook <u>Science and Health with Key to the Scriptures</u> by Mary Baker Eddy. We would be accompanied by a counselor to and from meals, and would sleep in our separate bunkbeds in the basement of the camp-owner's lodge. We were to write an essay during the following week defining what we had done wrong, what we had learned, and, with an apology to the camp's owners, to be read aloud to them at the end of the week. It was a powerful form of discipline, devoid of corporal punishment, but finding its intended result.

The winds of change in racial relations had not yet made themselves widely known among middle-class white children at Crystal Lake Camps during the 1950s, or even the early 1960s. Except for one very black staff member, the late Johnny Quattlebaum, whose employment was generally to maintain the horse stables along with other equestrian equipment, tend to various chores around the camp, and slaughter chickens for supper, there were no black or brown people at Crystal Lake Camps at that time. Johnny Quattelbaum's butchering expertise, which involved hanging a hapless chicken by the feet and with one cleave of his razor-sharp machete severing its head and letting it bleed out, could occasionally be observed by campers on their way to the stable - an introduction to the hard facts regarding food processing. What was not generally known was that this noble man was also justifiably entrusted to provide child-care for the very young daughters of the Camps' owners. One of the daughters, Anna, later married an African American, a very erudite young man from Detroit named Hal Jordan. Hal was dedicated to being of service to others, which he regarded as anyone's highest calling. Anna's parents were reportedly somewhat bewildered by their marriage, but accepted Hal without regard to his race. Many years later, when a serious illness prevented Dottie Alford from running the Camp's winter cross-country ski business, Hal took over until she recovered a year or so later, something Dottie never forgot, and for which she expressed gratitude on many occasions. While serving on the Crystal Lake Camp's Board many years later, I recognized that the clarity of Hal's thinking matched his passion for shaking awake a Christian Science population which was for the most part at the time blithely unaware that race relations continued to simmer in a cauldron of dispute in modern society.

Hal credits Anna with having encouraged him to step away from his career of choice – education. Hal's parents were highly-educated teachers, his father a graduate of Northwestern, where he had earned a masters in history. He had also been honored with an award for literacy by Barbara Bush, for fostering literacy in the Detroit Middle School of which he served as Principal from 1969 to 1996. His father was also honored by then-mayor Coleman Young, who was the first black mayor of Detroit, Michigan.

Hal's wife at the time sought to be Director of the camp her parents owned. With that motivation, she had influenced Hal to look past his role as a teacher, toward one as an educational consultant to school systems and teachers, (a career he entered, after abandoning his role in the classroom). That way, Anna had argued, he could serve with her, and they could both be Camp Directors. She reasoned that since Camp Directors' activities were only intense during the summer months during educators' vacation time, this would not interfere with his consultancies. This turned out to be erroneous. Anna and Hal divorced in 2005, and Anna passed away five years later.

Racism had appeared as a ponderable on the camp's radar in 1967. On February 8th of that year, then President Lyndon Baines Johnson had sent a Special Message to the U.S. Congress Recommending "A 12-point Program for American Children and Youth". Some of the specific language of that message resonated deeply with Camp owners Joe and Dottie Alford:

"We can, with the help of public-spirited organizations, bring fresh air and cool streams to the slum child who has known only a sweltering tenement and who must sleep on a crowded fire escape to get relief from the heat".

Joe Alford took this to heart, as it tracked poignantly with his commitment to the ethics and morals of Christian Science by which he lived his life and strove to operate Crystal Lake Camps; and although he was certainly public-spirited, he was by no means affluent; and so, in addition to camper fees, and modest revenue from off-season businesses, he and his wife had to rely on the largesse and generosity of certain wealthy individuals and organizations which operated at the periphery of the Christian Science church organization, not all of whom shared his noble views regarding race. Joe and his family vigorously pursued accomplishing the racial integration of the camp, but without the frenetic virtue-signaling characterizing, and often instigated by, the worst elements of institutional society. Instead, Hal Jordan used his considerable skills as a teacher to create a television program for campers, entitled The CLC Evening News and World Report. This activity taught children the basics of how to interview and produce news programs on a wide range of topics, including race relations. Integrating the morals and ethics of Christian Science into this activity, Hal showed how these might help campers better understand and elevate the discourse around race relations and other important issues. It was a worthy mission.

A very enlightening exposure to Native American culture also helped campers develop an understanding of the United States' racial history. In particular, the venerable skills and sanctification of nature cultivated by the American Indian was emphasized. Not too much was learned about the atrocities committed by both Native Americans on each other, and by the U.S. Government's complicity in obliterating Native American culture during the 19th and early 20th centuries. This issue was sometimes alluded to by discerning camp Councilors, but rarely elaborated upon in historical detail. A book entitled "Days of Destruction, Days of Revolt", subsequently written by Pulitzer Prize winner Chris Hedges and illustrated by Joe Sacco, was published in 2012. It clearly and unequivocally reveals that this complicity did not age well.

To support the emphasis on certain Native American values, the boy's camp was divided into four tribes, or clans: the Bears, Wolves, Turtles, and Turkeys. The unique positive spirit of each of these species was presented to campers and extolled. The last two weeks of the CLC camp season featured a series of athletic and skill-oriented competitive events among braves from the different tribes. In my last year as a camper, I was elected Chief of the Turtles clan, and won camp honors for most points, winning by improvisation : the last event was an unique triathlon, involving a quarter- mile run from the dining hall to a dock on Crystal Lake in the girl's camp, a swim to the anchored float in the middle of the lake, paddling a pre-anchored canoe from there the length of the lake to a small beach near where the tee-pees stood, and a 100-yard sprint to the finish line in front of the dining hall. A taller cabin-mate rival, John Stambough, Chief of the Bears clan, was ahead by perhaps 50 feet; beaching his canoe as I paddled my canoe trailing him, this friend made a costly mistake. As he hopped on one foot struggling to pull his sneakers on over his wet feet, I ran my canoe up onto the sand, jumped out of my canoe, and sprinted the last hundred yards barefoot. Joe Alford, witnessing this, was quite effusive in his congratulations, noting the shoeless finish and my flushed face crossing the finish line, and another cabin-mate friend, Kerry Joels, a track star at New York's Stuyvesant High School, who had taught me several track techniques, also exclaimed congratulations. It was the kind of learning experience a young competitor vividly remembers – that often, winners do the things losers are unwilling to do.

During my summers at Crystal Lake Camps, God was in His heaven, Eisenhower and later Kennedy were in The White House, the Mother Church was in Boston, Massachusetts, Sunday School was every week, and all was well with the world. Or so it seemed.

The continuity of values instilled by the Daycroft School, and solidarity among youngsters who imbibed them, was made unmistakenly clear one propitious morning at Crystal Lake Camps. As I was shaving the peach fuzz facial hair from my adolescent face, a year-round staff member, part of a local mountain family maintaining the camp during and off season, entered the bath area, taunting me about being too young to shave, and harassing me about wanting "to look pretty for the girls". In point of fact, I had at the time a very pretty girlfriend from Long Island, a camper in the girl's camp across the lake named Sue, with whom I visited during the breaks at mealtimes, when a brief mingling period was allowed and chaperoned outside the dining facility which both camps shared. We also sometimes briefly wandered off to explore nature. These visits had come to the attention of the bath-area harasser, who had been instructed to discourage any acts of intimacy between teenage boys and girls. He was a student-athlete, a wrestler in a regional Pennsylvania high school, and fairly intimidating. Just as this shave-taunting episode escalated, another camper, David St. Aubin, a Daycroft student two years older than I came to my defense, demanding authoritatively, "leave him alone"! Dave's parents had also sacrificed to send him to

66

camp, a far more enjoyable activity available to him than loading bags of concrete on the docks on Lake Michigan, which he reportedly did summers in college. Dave was a star member and co-Captain of Daycroft's football team, whose exceptional strength and athleticism was well known among our peers. When the wrestler half-heartedly challenged him with a grappler's gentle slap of the face, he found himself hoisted roughly off his feet and slammed into the wall. Dave's calm but resolute warning, "I said leave him alone – now get the hell out of here!" ended the harassment forever.

A year later, on a cold November late Friday afternoon football game as the sun was setting, Dave St. Aubin demonstrated in the closing seconds of a close game, what selfless team leadership looks like. With the ball inside the five-yard line, the play called was designed to enable Daycroft to come from behind to overcome a three-point deficit and win the game against a strong Halstead Academy. As we positioned for the play, it produced in me an adrenaline rush, which I had experienced previously, but never one accompanied by such resolve. As we hurried into position, I processed my role: at the snap, I was to fake a few steps to the right as if I was going to block for the older, bigger, powerful Dave St. Aubin, well known in the league for his gridiron prowess, He would simultaneously cross in front of me, deceiving Halstead's defense into believing that he was the logical player to take a pitch from the quarterback to score. What they may not have realized was that Dave would have undoubtedly relished laying some defensive lineman out; the quarterback, Jimmy Kohler, was on a blocking mission of his own, looking to block any opposing defensive player who might penetrate the offensive line. I was then to take the hand-off, look for the hole to be made by our offensive linemen on the left side, and score the touchdown.

It all happened so fast, and yet the memory plays out in slow motion. Hitting the line hard, I heard the oddly comforting symphony of tested masculinity, strong young warriors colliding furiously in oppositional intent, accompanied by a chorale crescendo of fiercely visceral adolescent perturbation, a referee's piercing final whistle accentuating the cacophony, signaling the end of the game. I lay at the bottom of a pile clutching the pigskin tightly, hearing the whistle, grunts and growls ebbing, vulgar pronouncements muttered in resignation. As I peered out of the pile of limbs and torsos atop me, I was informed by my coach's jumping up and down, waving his arms in the air, shouting as he ran to the pile, helping to pull us up, that we had won the game. Dave St. Aubin picked me up as if I were weightless, bouncing me up and down jubilantly. The sportsmanship demonstrated by both teams as we subsequently lined up to congratulate each other on a great game played by two good teams on a cold November day was palpable, never to be forgotten.

CHAPTER 7

Coming of Age, Sharp Contrasts, and the Influence of Romance

Adolescent development had been fairly normal through the tenth grade for me at The Daycroft School, at the end of which school year I turned 16. Child labor laws at that time required a medical exam in connection with an application for "working papers" for youngsters looking for summer jobs. The required exam was the first I had undergone since my mandatory vaccination shots at age seven, required to attend second grade in a public school in Williamsport, Pennsylvania. On a June morning following my 16th birthday, in New Rochelle, NY, a very pretty young physician, a woman likely just out of medical school, examined me. Although she was very professional and explained each step, I blushed with embarrassment at my involuntary erectile response during her check-up. The sweet mysteries of life were intensifying, testing the divide between the Absolute and the Relative sense of things not readily understood in the teachings of Christian Science, which would persistently escape my understanding until I was well into my thirties.

16 was also the age at which a conditional driver's license could be obtained in New York State. Both Connecticut and New Jersey at the time allowed an unrestricted driver's license to be issued to someone at age 17, but New York allowed only a provisional license at age 16, a full license available at age 18. This provisional license required that during the hours of darkness, a fully licensed driver accompany any holder of a learner's permit or provisional license driving a car after dark. My parents' home in New Rochelle made both commuting after daylight hours from school in Stamford Connecticut necessary, and driving to and from part-time evening or summer jobs without a licensed driver in the car impossible.

With mobility and financial responsibility came an intoxicating sense of independence, the illusion of autonomy, and empowerment. These coincided with the raging hormones of an ordinary, if well-educated teenager, steeped in good manners and beginning to understand the dynamics of popularity among my peers. I soon realized these qualities were important in many aspects of human development - including communication with members of the opposite sex. I was easily becoming beguiled when in the presence of women, without even realizing it; but a growing awareness that the lust of the flesh could produce pleasure began to call into question the very strict sense of Puritanical restraint which had influenced my early formation, even before puberty. During lunch breaks at Adelaide Hall, older girls with whom I chatted possibly discerned these things, and seemed amused by my attention to them. It appeared to be a part of what adolescent girls who were becoming women did; and it was an intoxication from which sobriety was not always possible.

Toward the end of the summer between my Sophomore and Junior years, during which I held a job in the newly-opened Finast grocery store on North Avenue in New Rochelle, I noticed a red 1952 MG TD convertible for sale on the used car lot of a Ford dealership on Old Post Road in Larchmont N.Y. I was able to cajole my father, who at that point appeared delighted with his young son's development, to contribute the difference between savings from my summer job, and the price of the MG; and so, another intoxicating flirtation began. My love affair with this classic car didn't last long, however. On the way to school one morning, the engine gave out. I and Gail

Reed, the quite beautiful schoolmate a year older than I who was a passenger each day, found ourselves walking to the next off-ramp of the Connecticut turnpike. Gail lived with her divorced father and her aunt in New Rochelle. Her Dad travelled a lot. Shortly after the MG's untimely demise, my father had negotiated with the Ford dealer, using the MG as a trade-in on a new, much more practical and reliable Ford Falcon two-door sedan. I turned this into a profitable enterprise, charging five other nearby day-students carfare, which I calculated was actually less than the train fare they would otherwise pay, with the added convenience of door-to-door delivery. My passengers noted my rates went up when I met a certain stunner of a young woman, who had transferred to Daycroft from a nearby public High School.

One day after lunch in the early Fall of my Junior year, I was chatting among a group of students gathered at the bottom of the beautifully crafted staircase in Adelaid Hall, which wound its way upstairs to the girls' dormitory. It was a fairly typical after-lunch conversation, focused on upcoming sporting and social events, peppered with inane teenage jokes, barbs and observations. From where I was standing, I noticed "the new girl", her long legs ascending the stairs with another student, her derriere wriggling involuntarily perhaps, but unambiguously under the form-fitting grey skirt of her uniform. Immediately smitten, I could not take my eyes off her. Almost as if she was aware of my interest, at the top the stairs she turned her head, casting her gaze on me, and, with a smile, winked at me. That moment sparked my first deep romantic relationship with a member of the opposite sex.

Her father was a prominent broadcasting personality, Howard Cosell, a profoundly brilliant man who would become one of the best-known names in television sports broadcasting. He and his wife had evidently decided that the environment at the public high school was unacceptable. The Daycroft School was of interest to Howard's wife, who was familiar with the ethics and morals of Christian Science, although neither she nor her husband were in agreement with the views held by many Christian Scientists at that time toward modern medicine; in fact, Howard was sometimes outspokenly critical of those views in my presence, which would inevitably evoke a sharp and immediate chiding from his wife. They had lost the only son of their marriage several years prior, at his age 12, to a disease which is today often successfully treated. The tragedy Howard and his wife had suffered appeared to leave him with a very dim view of religion generally, and Christian Science was no exception. However, he wisely left his charming and intelligent wife, Mary Edith – Emmy to those who knew her well - in charge of such matters. Emmy, the daughter of a government official in the Eisenhower Administration, once mentioned to me her interest in a religious movement known as Religious Science. Many of the precepts of The United Religious Science Church were similar to those of Christian Science, but without the controversies surrounding the medical issue.

As I became more deeply involved with this young woman, and more aware of "the outside world", I became more conscious of things to which I had previously never been directly exposed - "sin, disease, and death"- in the words of Mary Baker Eddy. The deeply spiritual elements of my early formation were regularly challenged in this new relationship by a very strong and somewhat mesmeric blend of influences, including the views of an array of people not steeped in misinformation regarding Christian Science, and who appeared to follow a fairly enjoyable worldly path.

By contrast, those loyal to "The Christian Science Church" regarding the very religion they espoused often unwittingly allowed misinformation and misapprehensions to compromise all aspects of consciousness. I began to observe at age 17 that their economic, political, socioeconomic, academic, scholarly, and religious views were fairly predictable. Denominational conflicts within Christendom, environmental degradation, and other issues were permeated to some extent by the ambiguities of what the "Christian Science Church" governance subtly imparted to church members. This in turn resulted in confusion about, distrust of, and no small amount of disillusionment with – including among students of Christian Science - "organized religion". A coalescing of the Absolute and Relative sense of things was not yet apparent to me.

As a consequence, my relationship with this young woman presented many issues which a boy raised within the ever-present influence of Christian Science might never experience. When one of my new girlfriend's former public-school classmates committed suicide, I began to recognize the Daycroft world as distinctly different than the world of public schools. During a period when most teenagers are quite impressionable, I faced a bewildering series of events, an array of things which demanded deep contemplation of differences usually reserved for the adult world. It would be years before these differences became a coherent understanding of how the world of human being works, and how an ordinary boy steeped in the morals and ethics of Christian Science could successfully reconcile and navigate it.

Having become so close with this young woman's family, during the summer between my graduation from Daycroft and my Freshman year at Rutgers, my girlfriend's father hired me to accompany him on a business trip to Green Bay Wisconsin. There, filming would take place for a television documentary he was producing featuring the Green Bay Packers NFL football team entitled "Run to Daylight". My job assignment was to keep a record of the film footage being recorded by separate Arriflex cameras which filmed the Packers at practices and scrimmages, team meetings, social gatherings, conversations with the great Coach Vince Lombardi, and players. The concise written record I was to produce would greatly shorten the time required to edit that program together. On the very first day of filming, I was introduced to an outstanding Director, Lou Volpicelli, who, recognizing my relationship with the Producer's daughter, gave me a quick tutorial on exactly what my job entailed. Observing my attempts to grasp the unfamiliar instructions being explained, another adult, a friend of Howard's dressed me down sharply for all to hear. He correctly asserted I didn't know what I was doing, venting resentment and warning me I had better do it right. While my first instinct was to punch his lights out, I showed the respect for adults I had learned since childhood at Daycroft, acknowledged his criticism, and quickly focused on the job at hand. Despite being enthralled in the presence of legendary players who dwarfed my Daycroft gridiron successes, I realized that I was there to work, not play, and that I had better figure out what I was supposed to do, and do it. I also noted that Howard took his friend aside and schooled him that despite my size and that I had just reached the age of majority, I was still a boy, but capable of doing the job. I had not yet grasped the unspoken reality of which Howard was undoubtedly aware, that the knee injury I had sustained in my senior year would likely put an end to my dream of playing football at Rutgers. However, witnessing these professional players working through late summer daily double practices, some struggling through injuries of their own, did give me hope and inspiration; as did sitting in the back seat of Paul Hornung's pink Dodge Polaris convertible with the top down one sunny Wisconsin morning after Howard had hitched a ride from our hotel to tiny Saint Norbert College, where the Packers held their pre-season training. Hornung's empathy for my desire to play football was a testament to the gentleman he was.

What would become one of my most vividly inspiring lifetime memories is of sitting next to the great coach Vince Lombardi at dinner one night at Fuzzy Thurston's Left Guard restaurant in Green Bay. The great coach's empathy and respect for ambitious young people was very clear to me, and his conversation with me, at my age 18, provided clarity and confidence like few other adults had ever instilled. He asked my expectations about playing football, and diplomatically about other possible career expectations; he emphasized how much work it took for even world-class athletes to succeed, and he gave constructive advice about training. Years later, he was quoted as lamenting, regarding a common injury in American football, … "The knee, always the knee".

Inspired, upon arriving home at week's end, I worked nearly 48 hours straight in the guesthouse at Howard's Pound Ridge New York home to have the list I was charged with producing typed in time for a production meeting early the following Monday morning. For this week's work, I earned the princely sum of $100 – a small fortune to a college-bound student at the time. It dawned upon me years later that most grown men with families would have taken the time off from work and done the job I had performed for free. More than anything, that experience introduced me to what true leadership looked like – not just in sports, but in every aspect of life. Howard Cosell, who graduated from NYU with a degree in English and then NYU Law School, one of the youngest U.S. Army Officers to gain the rank of Major during WWII, had in one week elevated and crystallized my understanding of the leadership qualities Daycroft had been instilling for 12 years. It was a lesson that prepared me for dealing in college with the results of the serious injury I had suffered just a year earlier at Daycroft, and with the adjustments a young man of very modest means would need to make. The young romance with his daughter unlocked hints regarding the Absolute and Relative sense of things, at a time when it seemed the public's perception of Christian Science had sadly become misinformed by a departure from the teachings promulgated by Mary Baker Eddy and her early students.

Re-connecting with several Daycroft Schoolmates years later, a fairly uniform refrain at some point in nearly every conversation was, words to the effect, "I'm not really into Christian Science any more". Exploring that uniformity in conversation, what was revealed to me was understandable disillusionment, not with the lofty morals and ethics of Christian Science itself, but with the governance of "The Mother Church, The First Church of Christ Scientist in Boston, Massachusetts". The higher quality of thought and noble life-motives expressed in those conversations confirmed something my intuition had suggested in my late teens: that things aren't always what they seem to be.

CHAPTER 8

On the Banks of the Old Raritan

"My Father sent me to old Rutgers,
And resolved that I should be a man.
And so I settled down, in that noisy college town.
On the Banks of the Old Raritan"

So sings the opening verse of the original Rutgers Alma Mater, the text of which was written in 1873, a century after Rutgers' founding. In a long-debated effort to eliminate the manifest sexism reflected in the first sentence of the original lyrics, written long before Rutgers admitted women, the Alma Mater was officially changed in 2013 to eliminate what came to be regarded as the misogynistic zeitgeist of 19th century American culture. The opening verse now reads:

"From near and far we came to Rutgers And resolved to learn all that we can".

The words "my boys" were also changed to "my friends" in the refrain.

In some ways, the updating of Alma Mater's words was a metaphor for the way my own worldview was very gradually changing. It represented how various reforms which the Daycroft School had encouraged, and had attempted to instill in its students during the 1950s and early 1960s, were taking place in society.

Until 1972, the year after I graduated, Rutgers College was, like most of the Ivy League schools throughout their histories, an all-male school. Academically qualified young women, mostly from New Jersey, who applied to Rutgers University as their "safe school", (to which they felt certain they would be accepted), had previously been admitted to Douglass College, a college within Rutgers - The State University, but separated in admissions by gender.

Moving from class to class at Rutgers often involved a bus ride across New Brunswick to the "University Heights" campus in Piscataway Township, NJ adjacent to the City of New Brunswick and Rutgers' Football Stadium. Most science and engineering courses were usually taught at the "Heights" Campus, although Rutgers' College of Agriculture and Environmental Sciences (now called the College of Biological and Environmental Sciences) required certain courses, such as Plant and Animal Sciences, entomology, and a few others to be taught at its campus three miles away, in New Bruswick. Today, the Science and Engineering campuses have the look and feel of a small city. The Liberal Arts School, Rutgers College, regularly requires a brisk walk of up to 20 minutes on the New Brunswick campus itself between classes. Freshmen at that time were not allowed to have cars on campus, but some students would opt for bicycles to navigate the distances between classes.

The sprawling Rutgers campus and bustling college town in which it is located has history dating back to before the US Revolutionary War. A noisy, working-class small city, New Brunswick NJ was known for a wide diversity of ethnicities, churches, Johnson and Johnson World Headquarters, numerous small businesses, significant manufacturing activity, and a significantly large population of

Hungarian-American Immigrant families, which had begun to arrive at the turn of the 20th century. Johnson and Johnson had discovered the diligent work ethic, educational backgrounds, and stable family orientation of Hungarian immigrants, and encouraged workers to sponsor family members and friends back home who might be seeking the opportunities America had to offer. The large New Brunswick Hungarian-American population was staunchly anti-Communist, epitomized by the large statue that still stands in honor of Joseph Cardinal Mindszenty, in front of Saint Ladislau's Roman Catholic Church on Somerset Street in New Brunswick.

Freed from brutal Communist captivity during the 1956 Hungarian Revolution, Mindszenty was granted political asylum by the U.S. Embassy in Budapest, and lived there for 15 years, unable to leave the grounds due to the communist regime's surveillance. His long stay became a diplomatic challenge, but maintaining that he had a constitutional role as Pince Primate and the symbolic leader of his country, he refused to leave Hungary. In 1971, a compromise among the Vatican, the U.S. and Vienna was reached, allowing him to depart for exile in Vienna, where he lived until his passing in 1975.

During Mindszenty's exile, he made at least two documented visits to the United States. During one of these, in 1973, he dedicated the newly rebuilt Saint Ladislaus Roman Catholic Church in New Brunswick, a few hundred feet from the Rutgers campus. My future father-in-law, a staunch anti-communist himself, and a pillar of the Hungarian Catholic Community, attended that dedication. Mindszenty had been made a cardinal in 1946 by Pope Pius XII. His cause for sainthood was officially opened in 1993. In 2019 the church declared him Venerable - a major step toward canonization. A beautiful young woman I met in 1968 at Rutgers had introduced me to the staunchly anti-communist Hungarian-American Catholic community, and to me figures like Cardinal Mindsenty show us that the cause of individual liberty is worth fighting for.

Some scholars contend that Cold War geopolitics and the United States's delicately ambiguous relationship with the Vatican are the main reasons Mindszenty never formally applied for exile in the U.S. I had learned the French word "détente' from Mrs. Serton, a graduate of Principia who held a masters from the premier language school Middlebury College, and taught French at the Daycroft School. Détente translates in English to "relaxation" or "release from tension", and was the diplomatic go-to policy term designed to keep countries from incinerating each other, and themselves in the process. I regarded it as a rather squishy way of tolerating what Friedrich Hayek first called creeping socialism in 1944, when he maintained that even well-intentioned policies could invite gradual disintegration of individual liberties.

The difference between the very small, nurturing co-ed environment of Daycroft, and the lively, sprawling, highly diverse atmosphere of an all-male Rutgers in the 1960s could not have been greater, nor more jarring for me, by then a young man. While the legal drinking age in New Jersey at the time was 21 - three years more restrictive than that stipulated by New York law, alcohol was fairly easily obtainable in this very liberal all-male school.

Rutgers fraternities were a major draw for many undergraduates between ages 18 and 21 in the 1960s. Rutgers held *"in loco parentis"* status within its student body, especially so with students living in its dormitories and using its other facilities, but commuters, once on campus, were also subject to it. Fraternities, as private corporations, served beer and other alcoholic beverages at parties they hosted. Some fraternity houses were quite charming, meant to rival the eating clubs of Princeton. Most had formal dining rooms, and compensated House Mothers, who managed to maintain a sense of decorum, civility, and order. However, situated on private property, *in loco parentis* presented a dilemma for Rutgers' administration, particularly as it related to its prohibition of alcohol consumption on campus. It was not unusual for fraternities to tap their first of several kegs delivered weekly on a Thursday afternoon, remaining on tap through the weekend. Brothers older than 21 could sign for hard liquor and wine delivered to the house, and there was little the University could do to stop them. There was an inter-fraternity council established to negotiate issues with Rutgers' administration, but it took growing public outcry about alcohol abuse to get anything done.

Rutgers' very clear and restrictive visitation policy for undergraduates living in school dormitories was also an example of Rutgers 'attempts to honor its *in loco parentis* responsibilities. Girlfriends could visit dormitories on specifically designated visitor days such as during parents' weekend, but when a non-family female visited – the students' dorm rooms were required to remain unlocked and partly opened during such visits. "She's my sister, and we were just wrestling" was evidently not an acceptable response to a Resident Advisor who might enter a room unannounced and find a Rutgers man atop his girlfriend. By comparison, while fraternity house culture frowned on such activities, actions against them were rarely taken, and all the locks on bedroom doors locked. That these policies were even thought to be necessary spoke volumes to me of then differences between the Daycroft Factor and the way Rutgers addressed things.

The young woman with whom I had enjoyed various activities nearly every day during my last two years at Daycroft had attended a small Junior College near Boston. The adjustment to being apart from her had been much more unsettling than I was willing to admit, or wished to continue; and so in large part because of our separation, and a variety of health issues including re-injury of my knee, I had withdrawn from Rutgers in my Freshman year, travelled to Boston and back a few times, returned home, worked various jobs, and took courses for credit at New York's New School for Social Research in the Spring. Commuting by train from my parent's home in New Rochelle to New York City each day, I was beginning to think I wanted to major in English, to explore my desire to write, and use the written word to make sense of the society I saw spiraling out of control around me, a society which deviated sharply from what my own early formation had presented at The Daycroft School. While taking a literature course at The New School, I enjoyed a brief romantic affair with a young French exchange student five years older than I, who introduced me to, among other sensual delights, red wine and Galois cigarettes.

I returned to Rutgers in the Fall of 1965. The extra year of life experience and scholastics proved quite beneficial, although the persistent knee injury problem continued to plague my athletic pursuits, in fact thwarting my desire and intention to continue with competitive football, and even Air Force ROTC. I also faced the interpersonal disruptions many High School romances experience. The romantic relationship with my High School sweetheart ended. Several of the girls with whom I was friends at Daycroft subsequently wrote to me, informing me they were not unhappy to hear the news; for all her physical charm and the enchantment which had so thoroughly beguiled me at age 16, my former girlfriend was reportedly not much liked by some of the girls of dating age at

Daycroft, who appeared annoyed by the perceived extent to which she had attached herself to me after arriving at Daycroft in our Junior year. Of greater interest to me at the time was the possibility that they might be convinced to have sex with me. Sadly, many of them, too, had attended schools nowhere near Rutgers; and my parents, unnerved and annoyed by my dropping out of school in my freshman year, instituted a "no-frills" approach to my financial support... as in "You're on your own". The expense of travelling any significant distance to develop a relationship with even very attractive young ladies from my Daycroft days was thus generally a non-starter. One, a very pretty redhead, was off to a small southern college perfect for her prim and proper upbringing. I had asked her to accompany me to a party to which I had been invited, after my having been invited to pledge a thoroughly Southern national fraternity, Kappa Sigma. Her mother noted her grandfather had been a Kappa Sigma Brother. I scraped together enough to pay for her train fare from Georgia, and a hotel room at the Roger Smith Hotel in New Brunswick, since razed and replaced by a more modern and elegant hotel, The Heldrich. Honoring her request that I walk her to her room, "to talk", which we hadn't really been able to do at the party, the Daycroft Factor made an untimely, frustrating appearance. Notwithstanding my best efforts and her willingness for adolescent foreplay – it turned out talking was all we did. I put her on a train back to Georgia on Sunday, and never saw her again. I was slowly learning that the sexual poison, once ingested without serious long-term desire or intentions, tends to short-circuit both romantic relationship depth and satisfaction. There was a lot of that in my college years.

The Star and Crescent

The Star and Crescent shall not be worn
by every man, but only by him who is worthy to
wear it. He must be a gentleman ... a man of
honor and courage ... a man of zeal, yet humble
... an intelligent man ... a man of truth ... one
who tempers action with wisdom and, above all else,
one who walks in the light of God.

Elected President of my Kappa Sigma Pledge Class, I began to understand and exhibit the leadership skills I had learned during my 12 years at The Daycroft School. The older Brothers, good men all, stated during my pre-pledging interview that they recognized a certain level of maturity and leadership in me, which they stipulated was a major reason for offering that I join their Brotherhood. I did my best to justify their confidence, emphasizing winning inter-fraternity sports competitions, and encouraging my fellow-pledges to utilize the tutoring sessions offered by exceptional scholars among the brotherhood. Kappa Sigma consistently posted the highest grade-point averages among fraternities at Rutgers, and the brothers intended to keep it that way.

However, the fraternity was not immune from the moral rot which seemed to metastasize throughout society beginning in the mid-1960s. Alcohol abuse and fraternity hazing at Rutgers had become serious issues, after alcohol poisoning and fairly dangerous activities became material for national press coverage. Fortunately for me, perhaps because of my reputation for throwing punches to settle disputes, most of the harassment toward me during "Hell-week" in the Spring consisted of having epithets screamed at me, which I actually found hilarious. In addition, each year, the pledge class was encouraged to stage a raid of some kind on the house. This tradition was thought to build solidarity within incoming brothers, and to develop an understanding of the power dynamic of such solidarity, to be based on the audaciousness and cleverness of the raid. My pledge class decided to pull off the raid of the century.

During a bitter cold snap in February, in an early morning operation planned by several ROTC classmates, we removed the front doors at 14 Union Street, hiding them around campus in the dorm rooms of willing friends who were not members of Kappa Sigma, along with the silverware from the dining room and kitchen; we loosened all toilet seats in the house bathrooms, coating each with a thin layer of Vaseline, arranged dinner plates across each of the stairs leading from both of the upstairs sleeping areas to the ground floor, disconnected the phone lines into the house except for the separate line into the apartment of the Housemother, Mrs. G, (who was aware of the raid, and tradition-bound to silence about it), removed all the lightbulbs, placed food-coloring tablets in each shower head, disabled the stoppers in sinks; then, we piled all the furniture into the downstairs living room, cranked the volume on the powerful house stereo up to its highest decibel level, and, with the incoherent lyrics of "Louie, Louie" ringing in our ears, high-tailed it back to our dorm rooms. We held out for a week before relenting to the Brotherhood's demands that we at a minimum return the front doors, under threat of being black-balled if we didn't. Having been required to eat dinner meals with our fingers in the formal dining room, and endure incessant vituperative harassment whenever we entered the house, we agreed to return 14 Union Street to the condition it was in before the raid.

The raid tradition, designed to build camaraderie within incoming

Brothers, and help develop an understanding of the power dynamic of such solidarity in achieving a common goal, earned us the begrudging but noticeable respect of a tradition-based Brotherhood. It was my first awareness other than my Daycroft experience of the power of cohesive unity - even when doing unpleasant things – toward achieving a worthy goal, in this case initiation into a Brotherhood steeped in reputable contributions to society.

One insidious aspect of fraternity life at that time was the chauvinistic misogyny which attached itself to so many young men oblivious to, or comfortable with it. It had remained a source of persistent conflict within my own consciousness, perhaps reflecting both my subconscious adhesion to The Daycroft Factor, and the more apparent brewing conflict within society at the time surrounding the issue. Added to certain unhealthy levels of self-pity and despondency related to my football injury, and the persistent sadness over the end of the relationship with my first romantic partner, it coincided with an increasing use of alcohol, tobacco, and meaningless sexual encounters. I began to eschew the serious scholarship of which I was capable, falling into a serious disillusionment and detachment from the purpose of attending a world-class university. The Daycroft Factor was on the wane.

In January of 1967, I again dropped out of Rutgers for two semesters, taking a menial job to accumulate savings. What resulted was a brief but important catharsis, allowing me to study the chaotic changes in society developing during the 1960s, not from the perspective of a student, but from that of a full-time middle-class wage-earner. Fortunately, my parents reluctantly allowed me to interrupt their "empty-nester" status and live in their home, although making it clear that I was to make my own way, preferably sooner than later. I travelled to New Brunswick on weekends to visit with friends, drink, raise hell and bed loose women, but soon realized my days On the Banks of the Old Raritan were not over.

CHAPTER 9

Where There is Love,
Religious Divisions Dissolve

Saint Ladislaus Church became the church in which a beautiful young woman and I were married on June 20th, 1970. As the Hungarian-American congregation largely moved out of New Brunswick, ultimately both Saint Ladislaus Grammar School which she had attended as a child and the church itself combined with Holy Family church, as the

Hispanic population gradually eclipsed the Hungarian congregation. Saint Ladislaus Church was to play a pivotal role in my reformation.

I had found accompanying the beautiful young woman who would become my wife to Mass on Sundays while we were courting to be a very pleasant experience. The services were strikingly different from Christian Science church services. The ritualism, topical homilies presented by dedicated but sometimes tedious priests, congregational responses during Roman Catholic liturgy, the practice of trans-substantiation convulsively controversial within all of Christendom, and my fiancé's celebration of eucharistic communion were all new to me, and I found them to be quite beautiful and comforting. Perhaps because of my interest, the Roman Catholic priest, Father Porgie, who conducted our *pre cana* interview and who later performed the Sacrament of Marriage during our wedding, had no reservations about marrying us, despite my best man for the Sacrament of Marriage having been Jewish. In fact, displaying a truly ecumenical sense of humor, he asked my fiancé's mother, in Hungarian… "Margaret, can at least someone in the bridal party other than the bride be Catholic?".

After the arrival of my son, my wife and her parents made it clear they wanted their grandson to be baptized in the Roman Catholic church. After some resistance on my part, I agreed, on condition that I be allowed to honor my own Spiritual formation at The Daycroft School. I insisted on introducing the elements of that formation to family and friends gathered to celebrate the Sacrament of Baptism at Saint Ladislaus Church. Researching scriptural Old and New Testament Gospels and correlative passages from the Christian Science textbook, <u>Science and Health, with Key to the Scriptures</u>, by Mary Baker Eddy, I chose readings from the Gospel according to Mathew, detailing Jesus's having come to John for baptism. Responding to John's astonished "I have need to be baptized of thee, and comest thou to me?", Jesus had instructed, "Suffer it to be so now; for thus it profiteth us to fulfill all righteousness". A correlative reading from Mrs. Eddy's textbook, stated that Jesus "knew that men can be baptized, partake of the Eucharist, support the clergy, observe the Sabbath, make long prayers, and yet be sensual and sinful". These and other of my readings were chosen to negate any doctrinal and dogmatic ownership the Roman Catholic Church might presume to have on my children's spiritual development. It was a useful compromise, as at that time my wife and I were divided about things religious. Fortunately, because my father-in-law was a pillar of St. Ladislaus Church and the Hungarian-American community, I suspect I could have worn a clown suit while presenting my readings, and the priest would probably have agreed to it. Actually, given the rather pointed rebuke of the clergy expressed by a few of my selected readings, they might have preferred that. By the time our third and youngest child was born, I had established very clear ecumenical views regarding the Roman Catholic Church. I learned this was a double-edged sword for most ordained priests, for whom most ecumenicism was only supposed to work one-way. The priest who later baptized my youngest child was appalled by my readings, but agreed to permit them, and we parted friendly rivals.

Born in Suburban Westchester County New York, from a mother who had left the Catholic Church to become a student of Christian Science shortly before I was born, I had no particular allegiance to any church. My father was raised as a Presbyterian, who supported his wife's religious studies. My becoming intimately familiar with the Roman Catholic Hungarian-American community and the Roman Catholic Church was the unintended consequence of having been smitten by a beautiful young woman who had beguiled me one summer night at the Rutgers undergraduate Student Center on George Street, known as "The Ledge". That enchantment had interrupted my self-imposed exile from Rutgers at a time I was thinking through the conflicts between what I had learned at the Daycroft School, and the events that followed. Many years later, I was able to resolve those conflicts in an act of profound ecumenicism, shattering conflicts, and embracing confluences.

I had bedded numerous young women while an undergraduate at Rutgers, before that enchanted summer evening encounter at The Ledge. The woman who was to become my wife three years later was an 18-year-old virgin who had spent as many years in Roman Catholic parochial schools as I had spent at Daycroft. Her sexual innocence was in sharp and stubborn contrast to the lustful adventurism I had enjoyed with young women previously, and my intense love for her, which developed shortly after our eyes met, was somewhat confusing to me. My mother had, after all, abandoned the Roman Catholic church many years before I was born. Her personal awareness of the scandals plaguing the church, and her previous resultant motivation to keep her children away from its influence, had changed by the time I introduced the love of my life to her: my fiancé was the first girl I had brought home of whom my mother approved, and without hesitation.

Our relationship did not sit well with my future father-in-law, however. John G. Rosta was a devout Roman Catholic, the only child of his Hungarian immigrant parents to attend and graduate from college. A graduate of Rutgers Engineering, class of 1936, a champion boxer, a water polo and football player at Rutgers, he had served in combat as a young lieutenant with General George Patton in North Africa and Italy. Returning home to civilian life, he was a founder of The Rutgers Engineering Society, and served as President of the Raritan Society of Professional Engineers. Among his professional achievements were designing the lighting of the New Jersey Pavillion at the 1964 World's Fair, as well as outdoor lighting for the rest areas along The New Jersey Turnpike. He was an ardent anti-communist, who had sponsored several young men during the Hungarian Revolution of 1956, and an exemplary member of what Tom Brokaw later called "The Greatest Generation". As Veterans Day approached in 1997, a New Brunswick Home News reporter visited John's home for an interview he expected to last 20 minutes. He was there for several hours. The interview became an early fascinating fixture of Rutgers' Oral History Project, sharing as it did intelligent awareness spanning 90 years of both New Brunswick and WWII. My father-in-law was proud of his Hungarian lineage; on Sunday afternoons, when I would be invited to dinner, the music of the Karanemeth Brothers, a local Hungarian musical group, would fill his home with the sound of cimbalom and other string instruments favored by Hungarian musicians. He played it loudly, and the lively, often wildly frenetic music had a pleasantly endearing effect on me.

I quite literally had to fight this man for his daughter's hand in marriage. On a chilly Friday night in October 1968, as I was picking her up for a date, Judy had been given instructions to" be home early". We had lingered after a party at the apartment I shared with three other fraternity brothers, and headed home near midnight. Upon arrival her father was in her face, demanding where she had been, what she had been doing, and reminding her that she was to baby-sit for her nephews the following night in Bloomfield NJ. Exasperated, Judy, a college freshman at Monmouth College where midnight was "early" when I visited her there, slammed her purse on the table in a clear demonstration of irritation and exclaimed: "God Dammit!" At which point her father grabbed her, put her over his knee, and began spanking her on her derriere with gusto.

I saw red. Leaping across the kitchen, I grabbed him and pulled him up, forcing him to release his daughter, placed him immediately in a full nelson wrestling hold, with fingers interlocked. Irate, I was later told I screamed in his ear: "you touch her again – I'll break your fucking ass!". For what seemed an eternity, we waltzed around the kitchen, him slamming me backwards into walls as he tried to unlock my fingers, my holding on for dear life with a death grip, knowing that even at 60, if he got loose, this former boxing champion would in all likelihood knock me out. As if on cue, Judy's brother, a classmate of mine, appeared in his pajamas, loudly inquiring "what the hell is going on" as he grabbed me in a headlock; his mother, screaming, grabbed him, Judy grabbed her mother, and the five of us ended up in a heap on the kitchen floor. I was getting ready to initiate a pugilistic brawl, when her brother stepped between his father and I, grabbed my shoulders, shook me vigorously and said "you 'gotta get out of here, NOW"! Man-to-man, I stammered "you promise me he doesn't touch her again, I'll go." "I promise", he said, and out the door into the chilly Autumn night I went.

I wasn't prepared to let it go, however. Shouting an epithet questioning both my future father-in-law's courage and his mother's virtue, I punched a perfect straight right hand through the rear window of my Ford Falcon. Observing the blood on my hand, I got in the car and drove back to my apartment, where I proceeded to talk and drink whisky with my friends until I passed out.

The phone rang a little after eight o'clock the next morning. It was Judy informing me that her parents would like to talk with me, cajoling my compliance with an offer of breakfast. Badly hung over, with breakfast an irresistible enticement, I showered and went. As I sat down that morning at the scene of the prior night's crime, her father appeared, sat down opposite me across the kitchen table, looked me directly in the eye and, with steely composure, said, "I want you to know I don't hold it against you what you did last night".He then immediately got up, put on his coat, left the house, got in his car, and drove away.

The enormous breakfast of orange juice, eggs, bacon, pancakes and coffee that followed was most welcome, as Judy, her mother, and I talked for several hours through numerous delicate issues involving our relationship. Her father later pulled up the driveway and entered the kitchen, inquiring bluntly … "you still here?". It was a pointedly unambiguous question. After an appreciative hug from Judy, exiting the house and approaching my car, I noticed something that would endear my future father-in iaw's character to me forever: this noble man had, while I was eating breakfast in his home with his wife and only daughter, gone to a junkyard, found a Ford Falcon rear window, and replaced the one I had punched out during the prior night's ugly stupidity. At that moment, he took over where my own father left off. When the head gasket on my car later blew out, he showed me how to take the engine apart, replace the head gasket, and while he was at it, changed the points, plugs and condenser, and performed several other engine-extending repairs. The car was fixed to be in such great condition, that it remained on the road for several more years. Observing the deteriorating condition of my leather-sleeved Rutgers jacket, a very nice winter short overcoat appeared under the Christmas tree as a gift that year. He tutored me in calculus. He taught me more about the physical world in which we lived than I ever thought possible. His demonstration of genuine Christianity was astonishing to me. He was a credit to both his religion, and his Saint Ladislaus church.

Later that Fall, my parents accepted an invitation to Sunday dinner in Piscataway, more than an hour's drive from their home in New Rochelle. The afternoon was delightfully reassuring to me, as any reservations my mother may have had about these people, their religion, and my new girlfriend, were completely assuaged.

On Christmas eve a year later, I presented my wife-to-be with a diamond ring purchased from my father's friend who owned Sylvester's Jewelers on Canal Street in lower Manhattan. The purchase was partially funded by a loan from my father, and the rest I had earned delivering U-Haul trucks between Philadelphia and Edison NJ at nights, an enterprise with which my fraternity brothers held a near-monopoly. Six dollars per trip, three trips per night. It was the late 1960s, when a loaf of bread at Shop-Rite grocery sold for $0.39.

With the encouragement of my sister Ellie's husband and my future wife's family, my return to Rutgers in January of 1969 was motivated among other things by a desire to gain the advantages which a college degree from Rutgers promised. Ed Czyr, my sister Ellie's husband, a successful builder in Ridgefield Connecticut, had advised me that I needed to get some business courses under my belt, and forget about becoming a writer. My future brother-in-law, Gil Rosta, who was an Agricultural Economics and Business major at Rutgers' School of Agriculture and Environmental Science, was also encouraging, pointing to Milton Friedman's tenure on the faculty, and the benefits of learning from some other renowned professors. In addition to having to acquire another 16 credits on my transcript to graduate, more than that number was required in order for me to satisfy significant math and science requirements, which were not my strong suit. Still, I decided to take the plunge.

While I found the change challenging to the point of exhilaration, I also realized with some sense of guilty regret that I was forsaking the hope which several Daycroft School English teachers had had, including Mrs. Hutchinson and Dr. Gault, that I would pursue studying the English language within the context of the Liberal Arts. My new course of study at Rutgers required much deeper knowledge of the physical sciences than I had ever imagined. The Daycroft School did not included biology in its curriculum during my years there, and, with the exception of Lynn London, a delightful young chemistry teacher at Daycroft, its science curricula was weak - certainly compared with Rutgers.

During his third and final year at Daycroft, one physics teacher, a portly Principia College graduate whose graduate work had been done at Columbia and NYU, once produced hilarity while trying to quiet us, an unruly group of high school sophomores, in his class. A student had protested that he was not the one responsible for some prattling; whereupon this teacher, who was nicknamed "Bobo" by students, shouted angrily that he didn't care who was responsible, but that, "if the foo shits, wear it"!!! A quizzical look immediately appeared on his face, he then turned and walked out of the classroom, leaving uproarious laughter, followed by worry about repercussions, in his wake.

My lack of experience in the physical sciences proved to be beneficial in some ways, but also immensely challenging for me at Rutgers. It soon became apparent that I lacked the foundation in some subjects which even most Freshmen, who were also mandated to take four-credit laboratory courses such as biology, possessed. I thus found myself competing for grades with declared pre-med majors, and never won that contest, despite many hours of additional study. While measured by grades I did not do well in those courses, I learned much, particularly about the DNA science surrounding the three- dimensional double helix, which James Watson and Francis Crick had recognized little more than a decade earlier.

It was comforting to me that what I was learning in my more challenging physical science courses at Rutgers was not inconsistent with the teachings of Christian Science as Mrs. Eddy had taught it. In fact, the distinctions between the Absolute and the Relative sense of things, much misunderstood and/or misconstrued among many Christian Scientists I had known, actually became clearer to me during this education, and likely clarified my understanding of the distinctions of both. From my earliest childhood, at Sunday School, throughout my Daycroft years, and other exposures to Christian Science, I had learned and often recited Mary Baker Eddy's Scientific Statement of Being, written in the latter part of the 19th century, and published in her <u>Science and Health </u>textbook. An exacting metaphysical statement, it reads as follows:

> *"There is no life, truth, intelligence nor substance in matter. All is infinite Mind and its infinite manifestation, for God is All-in-all. Spirit is immortal Truth; matter is mortal error. Spirit is the real and eternal; matter is the unreal and temporal. Spirit is God, and man is His image and likeness. Therefore man is not material; he is spiritual."*

Previously in my young life while reading her works, I had always regarded Mrs. Eddy's unusual use of capitalized letters as simply the way she distinguished references to Deity. At Rutgers, I came to recognize this writing nuance as the ingenious way she also distinguished the Relative, or human perspective, from her representation of the Absolute, the divine. It was a pivotal recognition to me.

Sadly, my mother passed away less than six months before we were married, on the evening of a semester in which I was to carry 23 credits to graduate in June, while working part-time jobs. I received a distressing 2:00am phone call from my father, informing me of my mother's sudden death. In shock, I drove at great speed the 61 miles up the NJ Turnpike, over the GW Bridge, traversing the cross-Bronx expressway, to my parents' home in New Rochele, NY where my father greeted me with a rare display of emotion, expressing his first in a progression of the grief a septuagenarian married many years could be expected to feel. A blizzard in the following days resulted in a subdued attendance at my mother's funeral service, even causing my father to advise against Judy or her parents making the trip, concerned about the dangerous road conditions. One of the more touching memories of that service, however, was the appearance of the African American custodian from her church, who braved the storm to pay his respects, tearfully shaking my hand and my father's, with words of consolation. My mother's wisdom, strength of spirit, and character which orphans so often possess, her lively sense of humor, and noble life motives have proved to be how I have remembered her throughout my life.

In the weeks that followed, Rutgers and my Fraternity Brothers sent their condolences, and a meeting with Dean Merrit was set to sort out the retaking of exams, re-scheduling of 2nd semester classes, and graduation.

The Spring of 1970 proved to be quite poignant and tumultuous. I had never known the passing of a parent before; I still had to work to prepay our honeymoon; there were violent protests around the country following the May 4th killings of students by National Guard troops at Kent State University, which caused many schools to cancel classes to quell protests - but not The College of Agriculture and Environmental Science at Rutgers. My respect for the school was enhanced by my Transportation Economics professor's unequivocal promise - that any student who opted out of the course's final exam would receive a failing grade – no matter how well he had done during the semester. It was for me, as for many students, a time of deep trepidation about the future. Like most, I was deeply concerned about the political unrest sweeping the country, but the joy of anticipating marriage to the beautiful young woman I had met three years earlier kept spirits buoyant.

The school year finished, I focused on my June 20th wedding preparations at Saint Ladislaus Church, worked to finish paying for a honeymoon in Bermuda, and planned with Judy for our future. We honeymooned at a lovely smaller British Hotel, the Coral Island, on Flatt's Inlet. Upon our arrival, prompted by my new bride's initial disappointment with the accommodations, I took my first adult stand against commercial chicanery, about which I had previously been quite naive. I had worked hard and paid in advance for a hotel suite with a balcony overlooking the inlet and the ocean; instead, ostensibly knowing we were newlyweds, hotel management had decided to place us in an out-of-the-way cottage behind the hotel. After my insisting that they make good on the contractual arrangements made by my travel agent, the hotel graciously saw to it that we had what I had paid for, and we had a wonderful time. They also gave us a service-for-six gift of fine English China tea set. Two cups and six saucers have survived more than a half century of marriage.

My views on human sexuality experienced a fascinating and unexpected insight during our honeymoon. To save money, I had opted for a European dining plan arrangement, whereby we were seated with another newlywed couple for breakfast and dinner. We learned they shared our wedding date, and were married in a Roman Catholic church in Massachusetts. He had played football at Holy Cross at about the same time that I was struggling with injuries at Rutgers, and so we enjoyed reminiscing about football. She was a very pretty woman who had at one time considered becoming a nun. Toward the end of our third evening dinner together, the groom pulled me aside and asked if we might talk privately. Curious, I agreed, and we retired to their room, where a duty-free bottle of 25-year aged single malt scotch had recently been opened. After a drink or two, with ill-concealed embarrassment this robust young man announced that both he and his bride remained virgins, that he was frustrated and needed some advice from someone who might not need any. Caught between the impulse to burst out laughing and the desire to demonstrate compassion, while utterly astounded, I quietly uttered "Jesus", and opted for compassion.. What ensued was a long conversation encompassing Roman Catholic theology, education, the sexual revolution and women's movement, various digressions, and finally the art of romantic love and sexual intimacy. Several hours later, his wife entered their room, saying mine had returned to ours, a signal easily understood despite the haze produced by some really good scotch. The next morning, both arrived late for breakfast, beaming, and wishing us a cheerful good morning. Mission accomplished.

Returning from Bermuda, I was able to spend my fourth and final summer as Waterfront Director at Breezemont Day Camp, where I also secured my new bride's summer employment as a camp counselor. As a wedding present, we were provided free housing for the summer months by Camp owner Jean Lauraine and his wife Bea.

A colorful and somewhat irascible Frenchman, Jean had served in WWII under Charles de Gaulle fighting the nazis, and had been imprisoned in Morocco. Immigrating after the war to the United States, he married Bea, a wealthy heiress who had inherited a struggling hotel in Armonk New York. She and John established Breezemont Day Camp on the hotel's campus, and served a wealthy clientele, including children and grandchildren of the prominent Sarnoff family, and Martha Graham's granddaughter. Children enjoyed a world-class summer experience at Breezemont, with the Head Chef at nearby La Cremailliere restaurant planning daily lunches for campers and staff. Jean recruited camp counselors from all over the world. Memories of his driving his yellow Chrysler 300 at excessive speeds, emerging from his home with a loaded shotgun during one of our winter visits to blast a pesky beaver interfering with water flow in the lake 100 yards away, or barking epithets with a French accent to staff, are memories which make my wife and I, and friends who knew him, chuckle to this very day.

As newlyweds that summer, we also found a lovely garden apartment in Edison, New Jersey near the Menlo Park train station, to accommodate both my daily commute into New York for work, and my new bride's drive to classes to complete her senior year of college. My degree would not be conferred until October 1971, as I was unable to complete a required calculus course until the three-week intersession of June, 1971, defining how I would spend my summer vacation that year.

CHAPTER 10

The Strain of Toil, The Fret of Care

In 1971, as throughout its history, the world of a Rutgers Alumnus was a world of work, not welfare. As one of my favorite Economics professors had stated quite clearly in the very first Economics class I had ever had … "The primary reason you are here is because you seek to earn more during your eventual career than someone who is not here". However, among other influences, the counterculture mantra of "Turn on, tune in, drop out" of the 1960s had resulted in turning the concept of liberal tolerance into the acceptance of deviation from norms, including questioning the value of hard work within "the establishment". By contrast, my earlier formation at Daycroft had always taught the dignity of work, the admiration of ambition, and a willingness to trust the United States government and its ever-growing power. However, my Rutgers studies had subsequently produced a seriously nagging curiosity about the events of August 15th 1971, at Camp David. President Richard Nixon and his Treasury Secretary John Connolly had at that time abandoned officially the 1944 Bretton Woods agreement, with Nixon laughingly responding to reporters' questions … "we're all Keynesians now". Nixon accomplished legally what his predecessor Lyndon Johnson had accomplished nominally in London in 1968. I found the events in August 1971 a significant, puzzling, and somewhat disturbing change in monetary policy, related to unsettling changes in domestic public policy, signaling as it did the specter of a serious upheaval in global financial systems. Specifically, the radical changes in monetary policy, by which the last vestige of financial order in the world had been severed, was in sharp contrast to what I had learned as a student at Rutgers. The ushering in of floating exchange rates, fiat money encouraging profligate government spending, and the vagaries of associated political agendas was of great concern to me in August of 1971. However, not uncommon among my generation was the need to put such esoterica aside, and focus on the practical necessities of making a living,

My fascination with economic and monetary policy was somewhat at odds with my love of history, art, music, and literature, that had been encouraged by the Daycroft School. These things were not then generally associated with the accumulation of material wealth. I soon learned that in 20th century American society, my education in economics, accounting, statistics, math, business management, and marketing would earn me a much better living than those things which the path I had originally embarked upon at Rutgers would. Fortunately, I readily learned the art and science of committing commerce. My initial compensation was at the higher end of the earnings scale for college graduates of that period, rivaling the starting salaries of engineering majors with whom I had graduated.

Initially, for reasons I did not quite understand at that time, I was quite uncomfortable with where my educational curriculum change had deposited me. I had been persistently recruited by a man named Mort Braverman to the Solomon Huber Associates in New York City. Solomon Huber was a brilliant lawyer who had coined the words "estate planning "as they related to life insurance in the 1950s and 60s. Located on New York's fashionable 55th street, between 5h Avenue and

Avenue of the Americas, Huber's firm was in fact one of the largest agencies for Mutual Benefit Life Insurance Company, founded in 1845 in the less fashionable Newark, NJ. Mutual Benefit Life would later fall victim to a run on the company of questionable origin in 1987, taken into receivership in 1991, and ultimately dissolved in 2001. But in 1971, Solomon Huber enjoyed a sterling reputation as an innovator, and provider of extremely valuable services to the wealthy, and those seeking wealth. Upon being hired, I was introduced to Sol in his office as a Rutgers graduate who lived in Edison, New Jersey. Seated in a beautiful leather chair behind an enormous crescent-shaped desk, he told me he wanted to meet with me soon, to learn more about me, and, searching his calendar, asked if the following Friday would work for me. To impress him, I quickly checked my recently purchased new Day-Timer, and replied in the affirmative, asking what time we would meet. "Six" was his response. Stunned, I asked "In the morning?" Eyeing me with amusement, he simply added, "take an early train". At that first meeting, Sol advised me among other things that if I ever needed an office in which to conduct business with a client, I was welcome to use his. I noted that the metal nameplates issued to all associates of the firm were the same size and shape found on Sol's office door. I soon learned that in Yiddish, Sol was 'fun der arbeiter-volk" – "of the working people". I greatly admired his success as much as the work ethic he demonstrated.

Among the services the firm offered, unusual at that time and incorporated into Sol's sales practices, was something aptly called "The Property Book". It was an actual high-quality bound notebook, a compilation of the form, worth, and location of various aspects of a client's financial wealth. The Property Book also outlined a client's financial plans, which were to be reviewed annually with a Solomon Huber representative. It contained separate folders for things such as wills and trust instruments, copies of other important documents, including Social Security cards, driver's licenses, passports, and the like. It was a unique and comprehensive attempt to popularize the central location of financial documents to the public, and it was especially impressive to attorneys and accountants serving the wealthy. Unfortunately, most of my "natural market" at the time – a few hundred friends and fraternity brothers from Rutgers and a few of my parents' elderly friends – those whom I could approach on a favorable basis, had little financial wealth, and little perceived need for the services available from Solomon Huber Associates. Nevertheless, to capitalize on those meager needs required a significant trained sales process. I did not see myself initially as "a salesman", recalling the disdainful tone with which Howard Cosell's wife Emmy had once referred to "advertising sales types", in telling us of a party to which she had accompanied her husband. At that point in my young life, I was concerned about other people's opinion of me. I did not want to be regarded with disdain.

My supervisor at the firm was a wonderful family man, Arnie Rovner, a large man whose father had worked long hours as a milk-truck delivery driver hoping to send him to prestigious Brandies University in Waltham, Massachusetts and then on to law school. His Dad had died while Arnie was in college, forcing him to drop out, and learn how to sell things, while delivering milk in order to support his widowed mother and family. Arnie's father had had no life insurance, and so Arnie had a strong motivation to sell the product far and wide. To him, every person was a prospective client, and Sol Huber's Property Book was a perfect ally. He was a very successful salesman, and I learned much from him, and from Sol.

Within a year after I had joined the firm, Arny saw that Solomon Huber Associates was not a good fit for me at that stage of my life, notwithstanding the extensive efforts expended to recruit and train me. A perspicacious and compassionate man, Arnie had apparently prevailed upon another agent, Mark McGorry, to befriend and encourage me. I credit Mark with introducing me to a delicatessen on the corner of 57th street and Broadway, from which he would order an unusual sandwich of egg salad and anchovies – actually quite good. Mark later left Solomon Huber Associates for some of the same reasons I later did to the same company. Eventually, driven by a common impulse among salespeople – to be their own boss – Mark became a lawyer, and opened his own business within Guardian Life Insurance Company. Arnie would also land at Guardian, after Mutual Benefit Life was dissolved, but in 1971 Arnie referred me to two other young salesmen friends of his, Brooks Komoroff and George Greene.

George was a lawyer by training, admitted to the bar. Brooks and George had left Sol Huber to start their own firm, a move that reportedly did not sit well with Sol. Brooks and George were in their thirties, both very bright, dynamic, aggressive young businessmen, and I was extremely taken with their energy and sense of humor, which I had come to appreciate working with Arny Rovner. I brushed off criticisms of perceived conflicts of interest which a lawyer might have while selling life insurance. To my way of thinking, applied knowledge of trust and estate law represented a confluence, not a conflict of interests, provided full disclosure was observed, which in George's case it always was. In addition, George was scrupulously ethical in offsetting any legal fees he might be obligated to charge a client, with any renumeration his firm might earn while working with that client. It occurred to me that both Brooks and George were well aware of how the recent swirling changes in public policy were reshaping the commission of commerce throughout our society, and I eagerly locked arms with these two dynamos, and did well.

George and Brooks confirmed for me that all things in market economies, from manufacturing to all legitimately compensated services, start when someone sells something. They taught me how to sell, and coached me through those first few years when every salesman regularly gets his head kicked in working the hardest job in commerce – selling life insurance - also known colloquially in some circles as "selling death ". Brooks and George were Brooklyn-born-and-raised in the morals and ethics of conservative Judaism, with which I was familiar, and they were very shrewd business people. Brooks was a graduate of St. John's University, George a City College of New York alumnus, and a graduate of Brooklyn Law School. They would sometimes good-naturedly tease me that I had all the markings of a perfect token gentile, known among more bigoted Jews as a "Shabbos Goy", who would help them build a prosperous agency; it was a bit of humorous truth confirmed during the Jewish holidays, to which I took no offense.

I also during this time learned of the excesses by which young people of all backgrounds enjoying significant newly-earned prosperity are often seduced, which can and often does compromise health. The cumulative effects on me of excessive alcohol consumption, the sucking of super-heated noxious fumes into my lungs, and a relentless work schedule which virtually eliminated exercise, resulted in a trip to the hospital one bitter cold night in February a few years later, and taught me a lesson. Shortly thereafter, I began my search to recover the Daycroft ideals I had put aside in my lust for worldly wealth, resuming the study of things I had learned as a child. At the bottom of our bedroom closet, buried under an ever-growing accumulation of clothes and paraphernalia, I found a copy of Mary Baker Eddy's <u>Science and Health, with Key to the Scriptures.</u> Reading it, I began as an adult a study of the Christian Science of my youth, which proved quite salutary.

As my health improved, I regained awareness and appreciation for the Judeo-Christian spiritual formation characterizing the Daycroft Factor. This helped focus my attention upon the moral and ethical light which often shined through some of the darker aspects of commercial activities in my professional life, and also the relationships within my friends and family. I was experiencing a renewal, which gradually broke bad habits and produced healthy transformation. This transformation also brought me face-to-face with a brewing major conflict within what I had then called "The Christian Science Church".

The conflict was discovered when I located and began to attend services at a Christian Science church in Plainfield, New Jersey, near my home in Edison. It was a conflict that would eventually be addressed in a court of law, and settled by the New Jersey Supreme Court. My joining the Plainfield congregation imbued in me recollections and realizations of things I had learned as a child. In particular, my attention focused on the continuum represented by the Hebrew Decalogue Moses had brought down from the mount, the 613 subsequent commandments of the Torah, and the ensuing teachings of Christ Jesus. These things had often been a source of goodness for me as a small child, and throughout my 12 years attending the Daycroft School, then again at Rutgers, and during my early business relationships.

With a renewed sense of health and duty, I put my shoulder to the wheel helping my partners develop what we called "a financial supermarket", intended to help clients with all their financial needs. In the aftermath of the landmark 1974 Employee Retirement Income Security Act, and driven by an awareness of significant economic and social upheavals in our economy, it was an idea whose time had arrived. The name of our firm became Economic Growth Group, Inc. – EGG – of which I became a junior partner, and soon thereafter President of Economic Growth Group of New Jersey. The New Jersey branch office was located near the first home my wife and I had purchased, in the tiny rural farm town of Dayton, New Jersey, a forty-five-minute drive from the Plainfield Church, and more than an hour's commute from New York. This also enabled me to spend more time with my wife and newly-arrived son. The New Jersey office which I proposed to George, who supported it, was located in nearby Princeton Junction, at 37 Station Drive, adjacent to the Princeton Junction station on the Northeast Corridor line. The occasional sights and sounds of trains at Princeton Junction from time to time unlocked memories of my dear older sister, Ellie, invariably bringing a smile to my face, and reminding me to give her a phone call.

One of my early stable mates, who became a partner when I did, was a young former Talmudic scholar, Leonard Mezei. Len had been raised in an Orthodox Jewish home in Brooklyn, New York, by survivors of the Holocaust, and had married an Orthodox Jewish woman, Bashi. An intelligent woman of impeccable taste in many things fashionable, particularly high-end furniture, Bashi had earned designer credentials then needed in New York City to accompany potential buyers into very high-end furniture showrooms. She also insisted that Len observe the Sabbath. He was said to spend Saturdays sprawled on a sofa, reading voraciously about Talmudic law, business, and world events. When he and his wife attended religious services or otherwise ventured out on the Sabbath, Bashi insisted they take the stairs, rather than the elevator. She also saw to it that he wore a yarmulke when he left their apartment in Brooklyn for work in the morning.

One of Lenny's attributes which I recognized early in our relationship was strict guidance by logic, motivated by ambition, enhanced by ingenuity. Lenny would hide his yarmulke behind a cigarette machine in the lobby of their apartment building, retrieving it in the evening to don when he walked through the front door. I doubted that he fooled his wife, who was fairly perspicacious. Bashi kept a kosher home, had a keen sense about money, and a dry sense of humor. My wife Judy and she enjoyed each other's company, when as couples we visited socially. One afternoon Bashi took my wife to a designer's studio in New York City, where Judy bought several pieces of heirloom bedroom furniture. When the two wives stopped by the office that afternoon, I nearly blanched learning how much money she had spent. To be fair, those beautiful pieces have outlasted most of the furniture we have subsequently purchased over the years.

Lenny and I became partners without knowing much about each

other's religious formations. Our friendship grew as management responsibilities were added to our sales jobs in our young firm, our EGG, at a time when my attendance at the Plainfield Christian Science Church was producing a rise in consciousness of things moral, ethical, and spiritual. When vacation time languor of August in New York City slowed business measurably, he and I would occasionally take long walks at lunchtime around Wall Street, and sometimes across the Brooklyn Bridge. Much was learned during these sessions about each other's childhoods, as we shared information and compared notes along the way. In particular, I learned things about orthodox Judaism I never knew, and he about Christendom. It brought us closer together as young business associates and friends, illustrating to me a symbiotic continuum which exists between Judaism and Christianity. It became an element important to me as we worked through various aspects of growing a business. I regarded as Lenny's strongest assets an unswerving ambition aided by acute business acumen, a desire and an uncanny ability to cleverly out-maneuver conventionality, accompanied by contempt for growing government impediments to business activity.

These attributes resulted in serious legal trouble for him, however, culminating in a New York Supreme Court Judgement for Restitution, entered March of 2021, some 15 years after we lost contact with each other. I became deeply concerned as I studied the case that a court judgement had seemed to be reached with no basis in law or fact having been demonstrated by the state. It appeared to me that the state was determined to abandon the rule of law in this case, as it appeared to have done regarding actions brought against President Trump in a much more high-profile case of contemporaneous vintage. I was indeed shocked by the *amount* of the Restitution Order, $980,990,038. In 2025, lawyers familiar with the situation while its appeal to higher jurisdiction was underway stated to me ... "the government's case is going nowhere"

In 1974, however, I had developed concerns I shared with Lenny about another, less esoteric issue - the somewhat excessive and irresponsible social behaviors we observed among various senior sales executives who gained financial success and newly obtained wealth. Many such salespeople were in process of divorce, and I learned that men experiencing divorce often lose their sense of propriety as things turn upside down in their world. During an extravagant convention at Bermuda's Southhampton Princess Resort, one divorcee whom we knew decided that the painful sunburn resulting from his Bermuda beach activities entitled him to sashay about the hotel one evening, displaying his post-divorce New York City sense of fashion, wearing an elegant, fairly diaphanous long white gown, without the accessory of underwear. Eschewing the grand center staircase in the Southhampton Princess's main lobby, he also seemed to prefer sliding down its highly polished cherrywood banister. These and other antics resulted in complaints to senior management of the company sponsoring the convention, who reportedly found such behavior troubling. At the time, we thought of it as a hilarious stunt, representing a New York City personality, and what I also regarded as the scourge of divorce.

Of more serious concern to us, Brooks's own divorce appeared to be pushing him away from the often tedious and relentless responsibilities of running a business. George, Lenny, and I met one weekend at George's Long Island home to discuss the matter. We came to the conclusion that our growing firm required fewer partners. It was a difficult, heart-breaking business situation, the first of its kind for me. Fortunately, Brooks's departure from EGG opened up a whole world of opportunity for him, and on balance, he flourished in numerous ways.

While Brooks's energy, creativity, sense of humor and overall *joie de vivre* was missed, that did not interfere with the proliferation of various services EGG was offering – property/casualty insurance, a travel agency, and an Enrolled Actuary Pension Administration company founded and run by Lenny, who recognized the Employee

Retirement Income Security Act of 1974 as a tremendous opportunity to add additional services, all designed to accommodate changing markets and significant economic policy changes emanating from Washington, D.C. In addition, the fundamentally flawed and profoundly immoral changes in the global financial system announced by President Nixon on August 15th, 1971 at Camp David became increasingly troublesome to me. George, Lenny and I often criticized what we saw as incoherent public policy, and how it could adversely impact the free conduct of commerce. My interest in these matters informed me that I was becoming wearily bored with the mind-numbing world of EGG. In addition, the arrival of the first of our three children was causing me to seriously consider a change of career. But to what field of endeavor?

One very bright light during my EGG days came by way of a referral from my best male friend, Eric Cherson, nicknamed "the whale" by his fraternity brothers at Union College in Schenectady, New York, where he swam for Union's swim team. A large but very fit swimmer, Eric had worked on the waterfront staff of Breezemont Day Camp with me. He had a few years prior to that lost his older brother, a budding major league baseball prospect, to cancer. I had immediately discerned in Eric a resultant deep and caring quality of thought, which impelled his professional ambitions in social work, specializing in working with troubled children in the New Jersey public school system. Eric honored me by serving as best man during the Sacrament of Marriage at Saint Ladislau's church. In addition to being our best man, he also became among my very best friends. I later served as best man in *both* his weddings. Eric's first marriage was to a Lutheran woman in an interfaith marriage, which ended in divorce; his second marriage was to a Jewish woman who had never been married. I learned some important things about interfaith marriages from his marital journey.

One of Eric Cherson's fraternity brother's wives had a younger brother, Steven Brooks, who was graduating from The American

International College, and was considering his career choices. Eric referred him to me in early 1974. I met and recruited him to Economic Growth Group, signing him on in August of that year. According to *every* woman in our office while I recruited and trained Steve, he was extremely attractive, and they envied his fiancé when he became engaged to Karen, to whom he has remained married throughout his life. Steve epitomized the well-meaning description of "a nice Jewish boy". For reasons I didn't understand, Lenny seemed not favorably disposed to this handsome young man with a winning personality, despite his sterling morals and ethics. Attending his wedding, I realized it would take time for him to blossom, but that Steve would become an outstanding sales professional, which he in fact did. Steve provided one of the few motivations for my remaining at EGG until 1978, but he left EGG in 1999, taking a number of key sales people with him, which did not endear him to George. Lenny remained solidly in charge of EGG's Enrolled Actuary pension administration business.

Once Steve was successfully launched, I decided to give broadcasting serious consideration, driven in part by an adult assessment of that field I had witnessed closely in my involvement with Howard Cosell less than a decade earlier. Enrolling in The Connecticut School of Broadcasting located 109 miles away, I drove there for training once a week, and six months later found myself knocking on the door of a trailer on Eagle Rock Avenue in West Orange, New Jersey. The trailer was parked in front of what looked like a haunted house with a transmitter sticking through the roof of its garage, but it was actually a television broadcasting operation, City of License Newark, NJ, serving the New York metropolitan market. Knocking on that door, as I had learned to do on so many doors in the early years of my sales activities was a life-changing experience. "Seek, and ye shall find; knock, and it shall be opened unto you" was the kind of inspiration my involvement with the Plainfield Christian Science Church had renewed in me.

What my intrepid seeking and finding had revealed was an opportunity that I considered somewhat providential. The UHF television station I had stumbled upon, WBTB Channel 68, subsequently went through a series of call-letter changes, from WBTB, to WTVG, to WHT – it was a dizzying progression of call-letter adjustments. The broadcasting operation had just been acquired by Wometco Enterprises, Inc, a New York Stock Exchange listed company. Wometco owned an eclectic collection of cable and Coca-Cola bottling properties throughout the United States and parts of South America. Wometco, majority-owned by the Wolfson Family of Miami, Florida had watched Ted Turner's successful rise in cable, and Louis Wolfson's vision had caused Wometco to seize an opportunity to get into the lucrative New York Metropolitan television broadcasting market, where homes in the late 1970s were still largely without cable TV. Wometco bought WBTB for a reported $750,000 in cash and assumed debt from the man who owned and operated it. Changing the call letters to WWHT, Wometco subsequently installed a transponder atop the World Trade Center, operating on channel 65; and with great broadcasting acumen, the Company also bought channel 67 in Smithtown, Long Island soon thereafter, linking the three via UHF technologies.

Things were changing rapidly in the broadcasting business in the 1970s. In order to justify its license, Wometco was required by FTC regulations at that time to devote a certain amount of its programming to news, including local news. I was hired to anchor a live daily televised program called Stock Market Today, and also a nightly 15-minute program called Wall Street Perspective.

My start on the air was less than propitious. The small studio in which all of WTVG's programming, including my broadcasts, were produced had been the living room of an old Victoria-styled house. What air conditioning there was, was commandeered for the benefit of the broadcasting equipment, not the staff nor talent broadcasting from the 14ft by 20-foot studio space. My very first appearance on

TV was hosting <u>Stock Market Today</u> live on the air at 12:30pm. It was surely one of the hottest days in August. I was instructed to sit quietly off-camera while the lovely Judy Bishop finished her midday news-brief update; then, during the short commercial break, she would vacate the elevated barstool on which she sat, I would replace her and wait for the cue to start my report. With the heat and humidity, I had removed my suit jacket, nervously sweating profusely, and was holding a gold Cross pen in my closed fist, while trying to push both hands through the suit jacket sleeves at the same time. "5,4,3,2,1…". My wife and friends that evening roared with laughter relating how my punching my fist through the jacket sleeve, pen in hand, came across on the TV screen, noting that I seemed very nervous. I recalled with gratitude what Waldo had taught me years earlier during the bugle bungle flag-lowering at Crystal Lake Camps some 20 years earlier.

WBTB/WWHT/WTVG program offerings included The Yugoslavian Hour and other ethnic offerings popular in the Newark, NJ area, African-American and other televangelists attempting to capitalize on the rise in popularity of the religious right and televangelism at the time, and the comedy series "Uncle Floyd" – an hour of hilarity hosted by the very talented Floyd Vivino, who had a significant following in the New York metropolitan area. Floyd would sometimes produce several shows in a row in marathon sessions, often into the early hours of morning, usually interrupted by technical problems. Some televangelists were rumored to be running a numbers game by citing various Bible verses by number. Several memories of comical episodes stand out:

- One morning, a trace odor of vomit wafted through the building, and I noticed a can of spray disinfect Lysol in the station's upstairs bathroom, reserved for on-air talent, who used it to get ready for their work. Evidently, one very stout and very nervous singer featured on the previous night's Yugoslavian Hour had "hurled", as it was described, in the studio. The little hand-written sign someone had attached to the disinfectant read, "where Yugo, I go".

- Another time, just as I was beginning my live broadcast, the portable three panel stock chart backdrop on the set fell on me in mid-sentence: it produced my first ad-lib "apparently the market's not all that is falling today"!

- One prank involved a studio staff member tossing a few prices of random iron and metal on the anchor-desk during my broadcast, as I was referencing the uncertain time a space shuttle was to land, estimated to correspond to the half hour during which the show aired.

- Feeling confident quoting stock prices during one Stock Market Today broadcast early in my career, "IBM was down an eighth, while Dr. Pecker was up a half last time I looked" escaped my lips. This caused the cameraman to double over with stifled laughter, as I blushed and corrected the misstatement to "Dr. Pepper".

- One hilarious fiasco didn't sit well with the station's News Director/Anchor Bob Fasbender, a serious professional who hosted the nightly New Jersey NewsWatch program. However, it demonstrated both the resourcefulness of those seeking to break into television at the time. and the hilarious unpredictability inherent in a facility long on talent but short on resources. We didn't have computerized graphics, but we *were* resourceful, and Bob insisted we do our best to look professional. A set of physical graphics mounted on poster board produced each day by a very talented Art Director, Tom Krusen, was stood upright on an easel, placed in sequence according to that night's news script. The set was held in place just out of camera frame by the station's all-around assistant, Wylie, a very tall African American man with large hands and long fingers. The main studio camera was focused on Bob as he reported the news stories; a second stationary camera off to the side would continually focus on the graphics. Manually, one by one on cue from the control room, Wylie would quickly remove each graphic from the easel, his hands out of sight, as Bob went from one story to the next. For whatever reasons, one night the graphics began to cascade off the easel during the live broadcast. As artboard graphics began to spill onto the floor, the viewing audience was treated to some tricks of the trade, as Wiley's frantically moving large-fingered hands frenetically tried to rescue and then recover from the visual entropy of random artboard spillage, all of which appeared, live on the air, over Bob's shoulder. One cool, calm veteran engineer in the control room simply uttered "uh-oh", as pandemonium reigned in the studio.

After paying his dues in this environment, Bob Fasbender landed a significant newsroom role at WNEW-TV in New York, and ascended to Managing Editor to that station's successor, WNYW-TV. He won an Emmy Award for his work there during the 1981-1982 season. Bob was a good newsman, had a nose for news, and I often referred to him as "fastidious Fasbender". I suspect he may have regarded me with some contempt as an establishment Wall Street type when we first worked together, but we developed mutual respect for each other, and had an amiable conversation when I returned to Wall Street more than a decade or so later.

The list of comical occurrences and unintentional sight-gags at Channel 68 is long. One of my prized souvenirs from those days is a videotape of bloopers, including some of my own, which are rich in hilarity. The experiences at Eagle Rock Avenue proved to be a sturdy launch pad for many television broadcasters.

It was a zany, eclectic environment in which to produce and anchor financial news, but one of the most enjoyable periods of my adult careers. When my on-air performances improved and viewership rose, I began to gain audience, and increased advertising gave me the audacity to ask for a raise in salary. I was also at that time contracted by Dow Jones to produce and host nightly news briefs, which were at first delivered to local cable outlets by couriers each night, before a microwave feed was established for a satellite uplink from Vernon Valley New Jersey, allowing national distribution. WHT-TV appreciated the additional production revenue.

I had also been lobbying for some time that someone on Wall Street who lived in New York be hired to conduct interviews there, as doing field interviews while responsible for two daily broadcasts and the Dow Jones vignettes each night was extremely difficult. Consuelo Mack was hired to fill the role, and we quickly became friends and colleagues. A cum laude Sara Lawence graduate, Consuelo had been one of the first women hired in the brokerage business as a stockbroker, seeing through and overriding the ruse on Wall Street in those days of placing women applicants in the secretarial pool "to start". Consuelo, who had numerous friends and colleagues in Wall Street, was a Godsend, conducting excellent interviews which enhanced our programs' content, and encouraged management to extend our flagship Wall Street Perspective program to a full primetime hour each night. During a brief deal with The Market Report Corporation, headquartered in Miami, Consuelo co-anchored four hours a day live with me, as well as contributing insightful commentary each night on set for Wall Street Perspective.

When the Market Corporation failed, Wometco decided to cancel Wall Street Perspective in order to focus on commercial production at the facility. Business circumstances demanded the business relationship Consuello and I had developed come to an end. I was devastated, and tried to persuade Dow Jones to hire her and join me in expanding the work I was doing for them. Dow Jones demurred, but I was happy to see her soon thrive on her own. Ultimately, we later both served as television anchors for Wall Street Journal products produced by different divisions of Dow Jones at different times. We remain close friends to this day.

Wometco's successful acquisition of WBTB/WTVG during my early days in television created for them an opportunity to deliver movies and other entertainment via small Blonder-Tongue antennae in the largest media market in the world. These small antennae, which could easily be placed in homes, quickly formed a subscription television distribution network. Wometco began an aggressive marketing campaign, and the movie network Wometco Home Theater (WHT) became a major financial success.

With the success of WHT, the company bought an abandoned part of the Wiss Scissors factory in Newark, NJ, and converted it into a first-rate production facility. The facility was complete with state-of-the-art control rooms, green rooms, a lovely cafeteria for producers, staff, and visitors; but there were no windows on the first two floors, a precaution taken by other businesses following the riots of the late 'sixties in Newark. The studios included a specially-designed flooring system, designed to absorb any vibrations from the factory operations across the driveway and parking lot. The television production facilities were soon in demand from a variety of producers in New York.

In addition to distribution agreements with major theatrical producers, the Wometco Home Theater offered a late-night variety program featuring pornographic movies and material, including interviews with porn stars. Production involving porn star interviews occasionally resulted in awkward, if titillating moments. Once, with minutes to spare before I was about to tape a broadcast for the Wall Street Journal, I had rushed into the makeup room next to the greenroom, customarily unlocked. To my shocked delight, there, in front of a full-length mirror, stood a beautiful, completely naked woman with a lovely figure. Stunned, I offered a gentleman's apology, which was greeted with "It's ok honey, I'm not embarrassed!", as I turned around and beat a hasty retreat. Another comical moment occurred when a nude porn actress, "Kiki" was interviewed, stark naked, in the studio. The heavyset, heavily bearded, bespeckled audio man was instructed to deal with the unusual placement of her lavalier microphone on a necklace from the control-room, without entering the studio. He was a true audiophile, and communicated with her and the production people involved over the studio speakers. "Please ask Kinky to say a few words for a mike-check" resulted in peals of laughter as Kiki informed him that she might be kinky, but her name was Kiki.

The television broadcasting business was quite a change for me, and a significant challenge from the standpoint of the human ego. For openers, because I had had no previous professional on-air experience, Station General Manager Ken Taishoff had initially feared I might fail, as so many newcomers in that field often did. He instructed Operations Manager Ed Kaufman to get me to change my on-air name. At first, I refused, and was referred back to Ken Taishoff. A retired Army officer, and a truly good man, Ken looked at my job application, noting the middle initial "B" in my name, and asked what it stood for; I explained it was Bruce, which name I had gone by since childhood. Noticing my first name, Willam, he inquired "How about Willaim Bruce?" The *nom de scene* stuck throughout my later broadcasting work at The Wall Street Journal. During my last three years in Broadcasting, serving on-air for The Christian Science Monitor's Monitor Channel, I used my full name, reflecting a culture world-renowned at that time for the integrity of its news reporting.

The early days of my unusual career change to broadcasting had coincided with my involvement with the Plainfield Christian Science Church, and my resumption of the study of the writings of Mary Baker Eddy and Christian Science. The mission of the Plainfield Church's activities included the practical application of its consecration to Truth, similar to that undertaken a century earlier by Mary Baker Eddy and her first students. I regarded it as a worthy mission. Championed by a married couple, Doris and Steve Evans, who were listed in The Christian Science Journal as Practitioners of Christian Science, I found it remarkably inspiring and salutary.

The organizational aspects of the Boston-based Christian Science church, and the somewhat abstruse nomenclature by which it seeks to identify itself, are arcane. Various designations, such as CS and CSB are code for listings of Christian Science Practitioners and Teachers in The Christian Science Journal. Certificates for these designations are conferred by the Christian Science Board of Education. Originally it was known as the Massachusetts Metaphysical College in Boston, established by Mary Baker Eddy in 1881. It taught Christian Science and trained practitioners and teachers until 1889. In that year, Mrs. Eddy dissolved it in order to focus on revising her seminal textbook Science and Health with Key to the Scriptures. However, having retained its charter, she had reopened it in 1899. It was established as The Christian Science Board of Education as part of the Church Manual, 88th edition, which she authorized in 1907. Some scholars maintain that this, the 88th edition, was the only edition she herself ever authorized. The 89th edition was published shortly after her passing by the Christian Science Publishing Society.

"The First Church of Christ, Scientist in Boston, Massachusetts", often referred to as "The Mother Church", boasts one of the most beautiful architectural treasures in that city. Curiously, there are "branch churches" of The Mother Church in Boston; but when one sees the circumlocutory title "The Mother Church, The First Church of Christ, Scientist in Boston, Massachusetts, this identifies what many regard as the 'official', or "headquarters" Christian Science Church. Article XXIII, Section 2 of the Church Manual specifies that the article "The" must not be used before titles of branch churches". Only The First Church of Christ, Scientist in Boston The First Church". Second, Third and in sequence other branches are not preceded by the article "the", a distinction made moot by the fact that many branch churches are closing in the United States.

The 89th edition of the <u>Church Manual of The First Church of Christ, Scientist, In Boston, Massachusetts,</u> announced to the press immediately following Mary Baker Eddy's death in 1910, just before her funeral, is imperceptibly different from the 88th edition, written by her. But that difference was revealed to me during a grudge match between the Plainfield Church and The Mother Church in Boston, a contest rivaling major schisms in Christendom over the centuries. arguably larger and more significant in spiritual scope.

Doris Evans was a dynamic, attractive woman in her 'fifties. She and her husband Steve had invested in residential real estate, including multi-unit real estate, in the Plainfield, NJ area, and rented many of their properties to young Plainfield church members. It had all the markings of a win-win situation for both landlord and tenants. Tenants were fellow church members who lived in comfortable, well-maintained homes, who didn't smoke, didn't drink, worked hard, and shared a desire for the renewal of Plainfield, NJ, not known as a desirable place to live following the riots of 1967. A resident of nearby Edison, NJ at the time, I was aware of Plainfield's reputation, and thought it admirable that the Evans' had established a niche which would not only provide housing, but have a positive influence in their community. I was impressed that Gary Singleterry, a young Morgan Stanley investment banker at the time, was happy to live there with his wife and young family. A very fit former punter on Harvard's football team, Gary and I often played tennis at some remarkably well-maintained clay courts in Plainfield. The Plainfield Church, of which he and his wife were active members, was, and remains, reminiscent architecturally of the New Rochelle, New York church, of which my parents had been members, and the Sunday School which I attended as a child while we lived there.

I had invited my wife, a Roman Catholic, to attend services at the Plainfield Christian Science Church, and a few social events with Church members, after which she shared her observations of dynamics with which I was unfamiliar, and of which I was unaware.

She pointed out that many of the women members wore their hair in the same short style favored by Doris; that they made reference to Doris's views regarding just about everything; and that they recommended my wife seek Doris's counsel about things in general. Having spent 12 years in parochial school as a child, my wife had zero appetite for this situation, and while not overtly interfering with my continued involvement with the Plainfield Church, even after our son was born, she made it clear she did not share my interest in the work of this congregation.

Meanwhile, I learned that the major schism developing between Plainfield and Boston was escalating. A former Plainfield church member couple had complained bitterly about Doris Evans and her activities to an official of the Boston church. This official happened to have been an authorized Teacher of Christian Science, authorized to give formal class instruction to students of Christian Science. He also happened to be *their* Teacher. The Boston church then set about breaking a key rule, which Mrs. Eddy had set forth in her Church Manual. Article 23, Section 10 of that Manual reads in part that no member of both the Mother Church and a Branch church … "shall exercise supervision or control over any other church. In Christian Science, each branch church shall be distinctly democratic in its government, and no individual, and no other church shall interfere with its affairs". In outright and flagrant disobedience to this rule, the governance of the Mother Church set in motion a plan to legitimize their action.

First, they sent letters to the entire congregation of the Plainfield Church, demanding that they fire their existing Board of Trustees, and elect a Board loyal to the Boston Church's Board of Directors. The Plainfield Church convened a meeting of the entire congregation to address the situation, and *unanimously* voted to reject the Boston church's demands, because they were in violation of the rules as stated in the church's governing document The Manual of The First Church of Christ Scientist, in Boston, Massachusetts. In response, the Boston Board removed Doris Evans's listing in the Chrisitan Science Journal as a Christian Science Practitioner, and later did the same to her husband Steve. They then demanded the Plainfield Church stop identifying itself as a Christian Science Branch church, pressing further that Plainfield cease and desist using the words "Christian Science" in the church's name. They went so far as to press legal action to enforce their demands.

The Boston church may have thought this would cause the Plainfield Church to fold its cards and go away. Instead, the Plainfield Church stood its ground and fought valiantly in Court for its freedom as a congregation to practice Christian Science as a Church. After nearly 10 years of litigation, in 1987, the New Jersey State Supreme Court ruled in favor of Plainfield. The Plainfield Church is now officially Plainfield Christian Science Church, Independent. As a television business news reporter for WTVG in Newark, New Jersey, in 1979 I had been assigned to cover this story for the television news program "New Jersey NewsWatch". My seven-minute news feature had evidently attracted the attention of The Boston church, judging from the phone conversation I had early in the subsequent litigation initiated by the Mother Church. I was with The Wall Street Journal at the time I received that call. Upon request, I sent a videotape copy of the report to Boston, and received a call back from a lawyer representing the church, who said he thought it was very well done, but proceeded to ask me a number of questions about my experience at the Plainfield Church. I was clear in my responses that I believed the Mother Church had acted improperly. The conversation ended shortly thereafter.

A variety of work, family, and proximity issues had caused me to separate from the Plainfield church in 1980. Shortly thereafter, wanting to share the ethics and morals of Christian Science in the context of congregation worship, I joined the Princeton, NJ Branch chuirch near my newly purchased home there. My wife and I had decided to share our respective religious experiences with all three of our children, who benefitted greatly from that approach. My admiration for, and affinity with the integrity of my Plainfield friends' stand, and in their resolve, has stood the test of time.

My on-air broadcasting career took a giant leap forward in 1982, when Dow Jones and Company's Art Pickens approached me to represent The Wall Street Journal on television. Art, a Chicago native who had served as a tail gunner during bombing raids over Germany in WWll, had then recently been hired by Dow Jones and Company to explore an entry into television. Art had been well known and respected in and around the television industry for his entire career, and my agent Bill Cooper spoke highly of him. Art told me that Dow Jones was planning to expand its electronic media activities, including into television, that my programs had come to the attention of senior management, and that they wanted to hire me to do on-air work for some of their programming. My excitement following that call was meteoric.

I enjoyed a nine-year career representing The Wall Street Journal on television, during which the Daycroft Factor manifested itself as a willingness and ability to write news and feature articles for television clearly, crisply, and with the polish of timely humor. Some of the best writer-editors and journalists of that time worked for Dow Jones. Among them, the venerable Joe Guilfoyle, nicknamed "The Iron Fist" was my first editor. Joe had started his career with Dow Jones as a "runner" in the 1920s. Runners would deliver freshly printed newspapers each day throughout lower Manhattan's Wall Street district. Joe refused to have a computer terminal in his office, preferring his Underwood typewriter instead. He retired at age 83, only because his wife insisted, and he was revered throughout journalism circles both at Dow Jones and elsewhere. The most profound statement he ever made to me, following my reciting both sides of an issue for a story was … "the Truth only has one side". Outstanding writers such as Pat O'Neill, Ed Klein, Sid White, and Ian MacLeod topped the list of those who helped me hone newswriting skills.

Joe and his team all worked under the sharp and unrelenting operational management skills of the mercurial Bill Clabby, an American Irishman with 10 children who had worked hard as a teenager in a slaughterhouse in Iowa. Bill Clabby, who in 1961 had been named Assistant Managing Editor of the Southwest edition of the Wall Street Journal in Dallas, rose through the ranks of Dow Jones with a sharp mind, strong will, and a nose for the truth. Tough but fair, it was said that senior management on the 17th floor of Dow Jones's 22 Cortlandt Street headquarters loved to hate him, because Bill Clabby came in solidly profitable quarter after quarter. Bill once chastised me for vouchering a $3.00 per day parking expenses at Exchange Place, which was the last NJ stop on the PATH tubes into Manhattan. He insisted instead that I park at Journal Square in Jersey City, farther away. It made for a longer trip for me, but the fare was only $2.75. So, I continued to park at Exchange Place, but only put in for $2.75 on my expense report. Because parking availability had become very limited at Exchange Place and the daily price was over $8.00, I made a deal with a young parking attendant, Michael, giving him the keys to my car in the morning. Michael would have it waiting near the Exchange Place entrance for me at 1:00pm every afternoon, for which I paid him $3.00 cash, but vouchered only $2.75.

Bill Clabby was also a sharp-eyed editor, who was known to pick up the phone and sharply chide a writer about the smallest error. He once called me the day after Ash Wednesday and sharply reminded me of linguistic intrigue, interrogating me as to whether or not I ever even opened the Wall Street Journal Stylebook; that while "Lent had commenced", "to whom money had been 'lended' was an atrocious affront, if not sacrilegious.". His rebukes could be painful, but he also had a keen sense of humor, and empathy for those under his management, particularly young fathers trying to survive the results of some very bad economic, monetary, and social policy changes since 1971. It occurred to me that having 10 children might very well produce empathy.

Bill Clabby reported to Bill Dunn, the brilliantly visionary Executive Vice President of Dow Jones Information Services, the ambitious leader responsible for Dow Jones's breakthrough technological achievements, including as original architect of Dow Jones News Retrieval Service. More broadly, Bill Dunn was largely responsible for leading the publishing industry into the Information Age with bold moves in the rapidly changing era of electronic publishing.

Bill Dunn's integrity had shone brightly when he stood up for me during a tense internecine meeting of senior executives I was invited to attend in New York City, transported there by the Dow Jones Helicopter from Princeton, a time-saving treat extended to me during that period. One of Bill's useful but equally treacherous henchmen also attended. I later learned this henchman was setting up the Princeton-based Dow Jones Information Services television venture to fail, currying favor with of The Journal's less ambitious New York-based attempts during an inter-divisional rivalry between the two divisions. When a comment by the henchman made me realize the treachery involved, I stared at Clabby, stating clearly and firmly the facts about the original plan, starting with, "now, wait a minute", expecting Clabby to come to my aid. Instead, Clabby sharply demanded "don't look at me – look at him"! Bill Dunn immediately took control of the conversation, beginning authoritatively with "In the original plan", then succinctly outlining the ways in which he intended to continue implementing the business plan we had shown would result in profitable television news broadcasting, worthy of the firm's reputation.

Bill Dunn's integrity is indelibly engraved in my soul, reminiscent of The Daycroft Factor, and what I learned from Bill Clabby's savvy business perspicacity has served me well through the years. Both Bills are gone now, but not forgotten, the source of their goodness known to me to be eternal.

My career track leading up to that meeting had included my on-air talents becoming quite polished and extensive during the frenetic media changes between 1981 and 1988, during which I had produced and hosted quality television, at a profit for the company. Programs as varied as The Wall Street Journal Late News, Consumer Update, Weekend Memo, Asian Wall Street Journal, European Wall Street Journal and others helped broaden the scope of my journalism.

Very early in my contractual relationship with Dow Jones, when Wometco's successors sold its facility to The Home Shopping Network, I was able to persuade Bill Clabby to save considerable cost by moving our production to the facilities of The Center for Health Affairs complex in Princeton, New Jersey, near both my home, and Dow Jones Princeton Information Services Headquarters located nearby. The Center for Health Affairs had ample available office space, which a friend from Rutgers had leased for his company start-up, and was willing to sublet for very little. It also had a Taurus Satellite uplink, which sealed the deal as far as I was concerned. The relocation resulted in increased bottom-line profitability. It also allowed me increased time with my family. I had time to coach youth sports and participate in satisfying civic activities in the Princeton area, including serving on the township's Recreation Advisory Board, where I successfully lobbied for lighted recreational ball fields, and the transforming of a former county dump site into a winter sleigh-riding hill for township children. Serving on the local CATV Commission, I was even able to produce and host *pro bono* for local-access cable the nation's first on-air youth sports coaching certification program, called <u>COACHING GOALS,</u> which earned a National Parks and Recreation award, a letter over President Regan's signature commending the volunteerism involved, and highlighting Dow Jones' reputation as a good corporate citizen. Mr. Clabby assured me all of this had nothing to do with his decision to allow the relocation.

However, the decision allowed me to pursue an activity in which The Daycroft Factor helped me excel. Like many parents, I recognized the benefits available to children engaged in youth sports. When my son began playing recreational soccer at age six, I was appalled at how poorly equipped volunteer coaches generally were. This became a key motivation for my production of COACHING GOALS. To make it a reality, and reached out to a friend, former Rutgers ECAC gymnast and diver Dr. David Feigley, who later became a professional sports psychologist and advisor to elite-level athletes. Dave told me of a youth sports pedagogy textbook entitled the AMERICAN COACHING EFFECTIVENESS PROGRAM, written by University of Illinois professor Dr. Rainer Martens. The motto prominently featured in the book is "KIDS COME FIRST". With Rainer's permission, I had videotaped several one-hour sports-specific clinics run by outstanding Rutgers coaches, including the late great basketball coach Tom Young, and baseball great Fred Hill. Dennis Meyer, an A-licensed Soccer coach in Princeton, one of the best I've ever known, also volunteered an outstanding clinic.

In addition to national recognition, COACHING GOALS taught me much about the game of soccer, and also about myself In the process, reminding me of the joy I had experienced in athletics at The Daycroft School in my youth. Coaching my son's team also told me things about being a parent for which there are no manuals. I also took training to become a Class 2 Referee, then a USSF/FIFA certification to officiate youth sports and adult amateur matches. Running the several miles a soccer player runs during a regulation match was in itself a reminder of how The Daycroft Factor encourages physical fitness.

The events on a soccer field in Staten Island, New York during a match played while coaching my son's traveling soccer team when he was 12 reveals another aspect of The Daycroft Factor: bold rejection of conventional authority when the welfare of children is at stake. The opposing coach had phoned me the night before the match, to give me a courtesy call regarding field location, directions, and to chat, customary in the days before GPS and email's widespread personal use. He told me the referee he had drawn for the match was "an idiot", an assessment which was hard to refute as the match progressed the next day. Patiently tolerating several bad and missed calls early in the match, one blatant error I witnessed not 30 feet from where I was standing was simply unacceptable, interrupting play and frustrating players on both teams. This referee called one of my players for being offsides. Stunned, but without hesitation, I declared authoritatively but respectfully "the rules state that a player cannot be adjudged offsides on his own half of the pitch". The whistle dropped from his mouth, he strolled over and showed me a yellow card, ostensibly for dissent, an infraction with which he was no doubt understandably familiar. Across the field, I could see the opposing coach shaking his head, and on the field, players on both teams were voicing ridicule.

Moments later, one of my players was intentionally tripped near the sideline, the ball going out of bounds without being touched by the offending opposing player. "Play on, advantage" chimed this pathetic excuse for a referee, giving the related arms-forward signal. Close to losing my temper, I loudly declared "There is no advantage when a tripped player is lying on the ground and the ball goes out of bounds; direct kick is the re-start!"

What happened next was bizarrely historic. This official ran over to me, showing me a *red* card, ejecting me from the game, screaming "that's it, coach, I'm sick of your bullshit"!. He then signaled the match to continue. My players looked at me, plaintively, and I instantly knew what my conscience mandated. I simply declared, "No way this continues – come on over here, guys". I was fully aware that it was expressly forbidden in the Mid-Jersey League for coaches to pull their players off the field because of a referee's call. But, as I cast my gaze on these disappointed boys, ACEP's motto, "Kids Come First" inspired me. As I explained to these players and their parents the reason for my decision and action, I noticed the opposing coach approaching with his team. He extended his hand, apologizing profusely. Fortunately, I had travelled the 40 miles to Staten Island with an ace up my sleeve. One parent, a former fully ordained Roman Catholic Priest married to a former nun, Tom Cusack, had taken the FIFA/USSF course with me, did well on the exams, and got some exercise officiating youth recreational soccer games. As we made eye contact, we both smiled. I asked the opposing coach and players if they would like to finish the match, in which we were ahead by two goals, with a full 40 minutes remaining. Introducing Tom to the opposing coach and players, all enthusiastically endorsed the idea. In characteristic attention to protocol, Tom dutifully re-checked both teams' player ID cards, explained how he intended to call the rest of the match, and 22 boys and their teammates joyfully played their hearts out, on a brisk October Sunday afternoon in Staten Island.

Later that evening, honoring the rules, I reported the incident and the results of the match to the league official in charge of referees, Harold Hussey, who had a great reputation for running one of the best youth sports soccer league officiating operations in the country at the time. After telling me he had never heard of such a thing, he asked *"you mean you actually red-carded a referee?"* We both laughed out loud, he booked the game as a draw. The Daycroft Factor had again blessed me, and everyone involved.

Back to the move of Dow Jones television's production facilities from Newark, to Princeton New Jersey: The move was also required to be signed off on by Bill Dunn, then Executive Vice President of Dow Jones Information Services, to whom I had introduced myself one day when we were both working out at the same health club in Princeton. Later, I had invited him to visit our new production facilities. There he met the award-winning television graphics designer/producer, the late Patrick Corbitt, a very creative man I had met while we were both coaching soccer, and whose firm, Synthetic Imagery, was coincidentally located in the same building as my production facility. I had hired Pat to produce our television graphics each day. A former Roman Catholic seminarian at St. Hyacinth's College, Pat was an extremely gifted computer graphics designer. As a collegiate seminarian, he had founded The Singing Friars, a folk group which had toured throughout New England, where he met a Mt. Holyoke woman who scuttled any plans Pat may have entertained about being a worker in the belly of Saint Peter's barque, becoming his wife and the mother of their four children.

Pat was something of a computer graphics genius and guru in those days, having worked with major movie producers and television networks all over the world after college. He always seemed to be six months ahead of the animated graphics images industry, producing such computer-animated images for 60 Minutes, the Wimbledon Television logo, the moving dragon for the 1988 Summer Olympics coverage on NBC, and many more for the advertising industry. Pat's work included using a then state-of-the-art computer graphics design tool called the Dubner, occasionally with which he produced beautiful graphics for my own programs each evening. At Pat's invitation, Bill Dunn sat with him a few times to see how it all worked, and was understandably impressed. Bill had arrived early one morning for a meeting, interrupting Pat's production crew's breakfast of Dunkin' Donuts variety. A health and nutrition enthusiast, after introductions, Bill scornfully joked, with good natured sarcasm – "ok, we can all now get back to eating DONUTS!".

One Friday afternoon in 1988, I received a phone call from Bill Dunn, the Executive Vice President of Dow Jones Information Services. He informed me that the company was sending me to Los Angeles California, to learn if FNN Chief Executive Officer Earl Brian had any appetite for selling his network to Dow Jones, and if so, for how much. I took it as a vindication: I had some six years previously brought to Bill Clabby's attention rumors that venture capitalists had just raised several million dollars for fledgling Financial News Network. I was acutely aware of FNN as a potential competitive threat to Dow Jones in televised business and financial news, of which I was an early pioneer, and I was decidedly not in favor of its ascension. FNN had begun to gain traction at a time when Consuello Mack and I were struggling, with the help of a very small support staff, to anchor four hours a day at Wometco's Newark Studio, at the same time we hosted the nightly Wall Street Perspective, and while I was also anchoring nightly news briefs for The Wall Street Journal. It was a grueling schedule. I had emphatically recommended to Bill Clabby in 1982 that Dow Jones should acquire FNN, and take the lead in this new media. In colorfully explicit slaughterhouse language, he told me in 1982 what he thought I was full of, and advised me to stick to my journalism, and that he would take care of business.

Bill Dunn's marching orders to me on that Friday afternoon in 1988 initiated my first hands-on experience with media investment banking. It also reaffirmed his bold ambition, vison and energy, and the dim view he took toward halting conventionality. Wrapping up the call, he instructed me to produce and host a videotape pilot of what a Dow Jones Television Network financial news program would look like. He wanted it on his desk the following Friday. Astounded, I replied as emphatically as I dared "Bill, that is not possible". His response to me has stuck with me for more than 35 years: "Do it anyway"!, whereupon he promptly hung up the phone. I was very excited, and extremely motivated. A brilliant senior executive who reported to him, Lisa Allison, with whom I was instructed to work, was put in charge of creating a business plan for this project, to be presented to the Dow Jones Board of Directors. A beautiful and financially savvy executive, Lisa walked me through how Dow Jones corporate life worked, advising me that this represented a competition between the Journal side and the Information Services side of the company, and coached me throughout the project. I was to martial my world-class team to write, produce graphics for, and produce a first-rate pilot production WHILE visiting FNN's headquarters in Los Angeles, AND to write a report on the trip for her, suitable for senior management's eyes, which she would edit into form and present.

I took an independent, highly competent engineering team with me to scope out the FNN West Coast production facilities, while tapping Pat Corbett to begin work on the videotape, putting him in charge of all aspects of the audio/video production, emphasizing his computerized graphics. I asked my dear friend and colleague Ian MacCleod to do voice-overs for the opening and tv-commercial replicas, and worked closely with Dow Jones Broadcasting Staff writers Ed Klein and Pat O'neill to finesse some news copy. Pat Corbett was to arrive in L.A. on Monday for a brief meeting with the engineers, before heading back to Princeton prior to my solo meeting with Brian. During the L.A. trip, I was struck by the difference in culture between the two companies. The FNN staff was generally much more casual-, "laid back" in California jargon, even by television standards. Female reporters were tan, trim and gorgeous, the men perfectly quaffed and full of themselves. The equipment was adequate, well- maintained and in good order. As I would learn some five years later in Hollywood after being nominated for a prestigious Cable ACE award … California, "the land of fruits and nuts", was different.

My meeting with Earl Brian in his Century City office was cordially professional, although he was dressed in business casual attire, while I had donned my best Brooks Brothers suit, starched white shirt, and military striped tie featuring Rutgers' colors. After preliminary discussion in a spacious conference room overlooking Los Angeles, he informed me the price for his Network was "somewhere around $260 million, give or take". I kept my best poker-face, went through obligatory perfunctory estimations and assumptions regarding cost and revenue projections, taking care to note his behavior. I wound the meeting down as professionally as I had learned to do. After thanking him, I left to meet with Bill Clabby, who had flown to L.A. with others from Dow Jones, to brief him on my meeting. He proceeded to sharply reprimand me for allowing the engineers who had accompanied me to overtly inspect FNN's production and distribution equipment, for which I took responsibility, but protested that I was new to this, and was working under the assumption that time was of the essence. His lambasting was his way of telling me that HE was my immediate superior, not Bill Dunn. I apologized, we had dinner together, and he dropped me off at the airport.

On the plane back to New York, I concluded this transaction would never occur, because Dow Jones didn't have the stomach for it; not that they didn't have the *courage;* but that they didn't have the *culture.* They seemed to prefer the internal turf battles in the raging war between print and electronic media to moving boldly into the new world of television. What I could not have imagined was that less than a decade later, Earl Brian would be charged with conspiracy and fraud for inflating the value of FNN and UPI in an attempt to secure loans to shore up the companies. He was convicted of the fraud charges in 1996, and sentenced to four years in prison.

Within a few months after the watershed meeting in New York, my agent, Bill Cooper, mentioned to me that The Christian Science Monitor was going into television. Noting that "those guys have a lot of money", he asked if I would be interested in representing them on the air. Recognizing that although my employment at Dow Jones wasn't threatened, the chances of further success in television there was quite limited, I authorized Bill Cooper to make inquiries and proceed to weave his magic, magic that had made television news names such as Mike Wallace, Roger Mudd, and other luminaries household names in television news. The contract Cooper then negotiated on my behalf with Monitor Television Chairman Jack Hoagland, who was to become a wonderful mentor, was sufficient for me to make a business decision. With the understanding that I did not have to sell my home in Princeton and relocate my family to Boston, and that all expenses incurred in the course my work would be paid by Monitor Television, I locked arms with Jack, and his amazing right-hand Executive Officer Netty Douglass. Having always put my family's interests first, my decision was made knowing how unsettling and fraught with risk a move of that magnitude would be for my children, ages 3, 7 and 12. Jack understood and supported me in this decision, offering that I be based at the Monitor's New York Bureau, at 500 Fifth Avenue.

This career decision was influenced by a gnawing affinity and commitment I felt toward the morals and ethics of genuine Christian Science instilled by The Daycroft Factor since childhood. These had been rekindled and illuminated during my membership in the Plainfield Christian Science Church, but also seriously challenged since I had ended my involvement with the Plainfield Church. My assessment was that all was not well with the Christian Science movement broadly, and I felt compelled at that stage of my career to closely examine the causes – if in a somewhat surreptitious and clandestine way.

Within a month, I had resigned from Dow Jones on the same date by coincidence that my friend Bill Dunn did. Handing my resignation letter to Bill Clabby, and engaging in conversation with him, was among the most poignant moments of my career, and my life. Bill Clabby stated that the firm was losing a really good man, and that the Monitor was gaining one. Holding back tears while shaking hands with Bill for the last time was difficult. In 1992, serving in an *ad hoc* investment banking capacity on behalf of The Christian Science Publishing Society, I was delighted to retain Bill Dunn as a consultant during an initiative to salvage remnants of The Monitor Channel. His insights regarding technology and the Information Age he helped usher in to our society, were extreme useful.

Bill Clabby left this earth in 1997. Bill Dunn later became a good client of Morgan Stanley, passing away in 2023, shortly after I retired from Morgan Stanley. Both men were the backbone of a news and information company, Dow Jones, still regarded by many as a premier news organization.

I spent the three years between 1989 and 1992 reporting for Monitor Television, a broadcast publication of The Christian Science Monitor. Based at its 5th Avenue location, where a small advertising staff also worked, I broadcast Monday through Thursday after the close of trading from the New York Stock Exchange television gallery, overlooking the trading floor. During that activity, I met a CNN producer, Maria Bartiromo, who worked from the glass booth adjoining the Monitor's booth on the Second floor. I admired Maria as a delightful and strong professional woman, who today I regard as one of the greatest professional journalists, on or off Wall Street, of our time.

My schedule in service to The Monitor Channel was a full one. Each day, after covering stories Monday through Thursday evening, I flew to Boston early on Friday mornings to tape my award-winning program "Money and You", which aired several times throughout the weekend, beginning Friday evening during prime time. Also on Fridays, I appeared live on the set with Lynde McCormick, who hosted the nightly Monitor Channel program "Business Byline", which Monday through Thursday included my nightly broadcasts from the New York Stock Exchange. A great producer, Mike Cahill, at Monitor Television's state-of-the art Boston studios, kept me on track throughout the week, with daily telephone conversations about content, as well as happenings at the Church Center in Boston. I also hired a young writer, Tim McGorry, to assist me and Mike from New York, necessitated by my hectic schedule. Occasionally, I also reported for the award-winning international Monitor Radio News Reports, using broadcasting facilities at the United Nations building overlooking the East River, into which I occasionally mused it should be tipped.

The Daycroft Factor had resonated noticeably when I first reported for duty to Monitor Television on a very hot, humid day in August, 1989. Looking out the window of the Back Bay Hilton overlooking the architecturally splendid Christian Science Center complex, some very powerful emotions welled up, ranging from humble gratitude for my parents' homely succession of sacrifices and toils in my early youth, to angry resolve that whatever had so subverted the teachings of Mary Baker Eddy could be rooted out by the success of The Monitor Channel. It took on a kind of Mission Impossible ambience, marked by quiet resolve, alertness to duty. and adherence to the strict journalistic and business standards I had learned at Dow Jones. During my three years' service to Monitor Television, it often occurred to me that the only thing more horrific than feeding a Christian to the lions might be feeding a lion to the Christians.

I had been given instructions by my mentor Jack Hogland that I should familiarize myself with the Christian Science Publishing Society facilities, old and new, as soon as possible upon my arrival. In particular, I was to acquaint myself with the television operations, in order to recognize the synergies planned between print and electronic publishing. The design and layout for newsroom activities for television production and Monitor Radio studios were quite impressive, reflecting a great deal of constructive thought and planning by a remarkable woman, Netty Douglass, who had been picked by the visionary Jack Hoagland.

So, at about 5:15pm, after registering at the hotel, I walked the half-block or so to the Belvidere Street side-entrance for employees. Pushing the communications unit button on the wall unit to have someone, presumably from security, unlock the door for me, a voice came from the unit's intercom, politely inquiring the nature of my visit. There was a brief pause after I identified myself, adding "I work here now". The response, "Sir, we close at 4:30", caused me to burst out laughing, punctuated by my assertion "I think that's about to change!". After a moment, the buzzer sounded, and I opened the door and stepped inside, the air conditioning a refreshing relief from the beastly Back Bay heat and humidity which often prompted people to go on vacation in August. As I walked through the vast, long broadcasting colonnade building designed by I.M. Pei in the 1970s, to the old Publishing Society building, built in 1934, I regarded my walk as something of a conundrum: I was surveilling a magnificently beautiful production building, in which essentially no one was at work. That, too, was about to change.

The colonnade building was attached to the original publishing house by a long wood-floored corridor adjacent to the original printing presses, which, with excellent regular maintenance and upgrades, were still in full operation. Walking this corridor and watching the printing presses rolling out the daily international Christin Science Monitor newspaper, the pungently pleasant odor of printer's ink reminded me metaphorically of the publishing era I was exiting, and the new one which had emerged on my watch, and rapidly changing. I soon learned that the newsroom wars between print and electronic publishing which I had observed while at The Wall Street Journal were reaching into the staid newsrooms of The Christian Science Monitor, but with the added incendiary influence of religiosity.

As important to me as the Monitor's place in journalism were several historical events which had piqued my interest previously. One was the events following Mary Baker's death in December 1910, culminating in what came to be known in some circles as "The Great Litigation" between 1919 and 1921. During my work for Monitor Television, I discovered the purpose and results of that litigation had become one of the Christian Science movement's best-kept dirty little secrets. In combination with other departures from both the letter and the spirit of Mrs. Eddy's instructions, I concluded it had sown the seeds of the organization's gradual decline. There was also the matter of largely imperceptible changes in the <u>Manual of the Mother Church</u> immediately after Mrs. Eddy's passing.

The more contemporaneous specter of internecine news business controversies required little research at the time, or since. As the development of electronic publishing became unavoidable in the 1970s and 1980s, Kay Fanning, an heiress-turned-Monitor newspaper Editor-in-Chief, was said to be quite unhappy with the Christian Science Church Board of Directors' decision to commit significant resources to The Monitor's proposed entry into television, at the expense of the print newspaper. They had tapped Jack Hoagland to lead that mission. Mrs. Fanning in fact had left the Christian Science Monitor in 1988, and became a Director with the Boston Globe in 1990. The Globe reportedly took a wary view of their Boston rival's previous purchase of Boston's WQTV, Channel 68, in 1986.

The curious polity within the Church organization ultimately caused the discontinuance of the Monitor Television initiatives. On Monday, March 2, 1992, the news of the decision to shut Monitor Television down hit the front pages of newspapers. That morning, I received a call from a friend, the CEO of a major investment house which had recently launched a struggling media limited partnership, asking me what was happening. After giving him the details, I asked dejectedly, "You want to buy a television network?" His gallows humor response was what one might expect from a friend, a seasoned Wall Street icon known for his sense of humor: "yeah, but probably not yours!" He did arrange for me to meet with his firm's chief media investment banker, which brightened an otherwise somber day. Later, following the most bizarre few months I could imagine, we agreed that I should be working with Merrill Lynch.

After March of 1992, I stayed on to help Jack Hoagland and Netty Douglass navigate the consequences of Board of Directors' decision, I gradually realized there was diminishing reality in salvaging The Monitor Channel. The Board of Directors of The Mother Church, The First Church of Christ, Scientist in Boston Massachusetts, wanted it killed, dead. The long knives were out, and, as the saying goes, the inmates were running the asylum. One particularly preposterous, somewhat surreal scenario which developed was particularly troublesome. *Pro tempore* manager of the Christian Science Publishing Society Al Carnesciali, an authorized Teacher of Christian Science, required that I work with two "Christian Scientists". One was a management consultant, a Dartmouth graduate who also held an MBA from MIT's Sloan School, Miles Harbur. The other, 32-year-old Eric Resteiner, held no such credentials. Eric had bragged to me about dropping out of The University of Michigan because, in his words, "they were all idiots". Eric's credentials were a glib personality, his listing as a Christian Science Practitioner in The Christian Science Journal, and his being a student of Al Carnesciali. My first impression upon being introduced to him in the executive offices of the Christian Science Publishing Society was that he had a great tan, straight white teeth, and a crooked smile. He was wearing tan khaki trousers, a shirt and blazer with no tie, and no socks.

It was hard not to like Eric, who had the outward markings of a charming and savvy young man. Miles and I tolerated his manifestly juvenile behavior, because his involvement came not as a request, but as a requirement. He was thoroughly unequipped to do the tedious, nitty-gritty work of business planning - crunching numbers, testing assumptions, and related work. Holding him at arm's length as Miles and I worked to pull together a business plan, I became increasingly intrigued as to just what Eric's intentions were. He seemed a sincere student of Christian Science. However, his behavior suggested he had recast, through his own interpretive lens, the title of Mary Baker Eddy's denominational textbook <u>Science and Health with Key to the Scriptures</u>, to *Signs of Wealth with Ease to the Strictures*.

In the summer of 1992, during a presentation of the business plan Miles and I had developed, a staffer had handed me a note attached to a newswire item: the Board had sold the satellite transponder, a key asset involved in the plan, out from under us. Despite Eric's desire and persistent efforts, I realized the *game was over. The mandarins of the Christian Science Church wanted the Monitor Channel killed, dead.* Even Eric's insistent persistence, which I felt morally obligated to support professionally for a while, couldn't change that manifestly apparent fact.

Nor could it forever hide Eric's criminal intentions and actions, which, thanks to both intuition and experience, I later observed after returning to Wall Street. In 2007, long after I disassociated myself from Eric Resteiner, long after alerting a member of the Christian Science Board of Directors to beware of alarming reports I had heard from various Christian Scientists, I learned that Eric Resteiner was sentenced to 87 months in federal prison, followed by two years of supervised release following incarceration, and deportation from the United States after that, for orchestrating a fraudulent investment scheme that had defrauded investors, many of them Christian Scientists, out of over $30,000,000. Zeitgeist is reflected in the ingenious use of then nascent internet technology by those defrauded, to expose his lavish lifestyle, featuring luxury vehicles, a yacht, a private jet, and multiple homes around the world.

Miles Harbur, who had plausibly been taken in by Eric's bravado and continued listing in the Christian Science Journal as a Christian Science Practitioner, was directly implicated and charged in connection with Eric's nefarious activities. He consented to a financial judgement that included being held liable for $1,100,000 in disgorgement, though payment was reportedly waived due to his financial condition.

During my youth at the Daycroft School, and also from conversations with my favorite camp councilor David "Waldo" Purdy, I had been taught the value of human intuition, and how often in history intuition has proved to be a superior human faculty than reason – particularly in the sciences, where Copernicus's intuitions regarding heliocentricity paved the way for Galileo, who suffered condemnation for his work. As an adult while attending the Plainfield Christian Science church, I had studied the works of Bicknell Young, C.S.B., who had been a student of Edward Kimball, one of Mrs. Eddy's most trusted students and a key figure in the early Christian Science movement. His declarative passage, deeply rooted in the Absolute sense of things, reads as follows:

"There is no such thing as an incurable disease.
There is no such thing as an unforgivable sin.
There is no such thing as ' it's too late' ".

While I never quoted this to either of them, I remained hopeful that the essence of this would provide some sense of salvation for both Eric and Miles.

One night in the weeks following my summer's work to salvage the

Monitor Channel, I had a long and deep conversation with a dear, devout Roman Catholic friend in Wall Street, John Abbracciamento, who happened to be my very savvy Merrill Lynch Financial Consultant. Following that conversation, the notion *"right religion; wrong church"* recurred to me often.

My agent Bill Cooper soon arranged for me to meet with major broadcasting executives as I contemplated staying in broadcasting, versus what to do with the rest of my life. During these meetings, and in working on an independent project at The New York Stock Exchange, the thought "right religion, wrong church" regularly repeated itself, possibly fanned by resentment, but also by a deep, lifelong devotion to The Daycroft Factor, and the consecration to the goodness of the Christ it established. Those responsible for hiring seemed much more interested in learning if I "was a Christian Scientist", (usually accompanied by what was to them the related question "did I go to doctors"?) and "what really happened to The Monitor Channel" and about its relationship with the Christian Science church, than my considerable contributions to broadcast journalism. It occurred to me that I had had a good run in broadcasting since the days I had pioneered business and financial news on television, and that all indications were that the market was telling me something. Discouraged, but needing to support my wife and family, I returned to Wall Street as a Financial Advisor.

Shortly after signing on with Merrill Lynch, on February 26th, 1993, a bomb exploded in a parking area under the World Trade Center's North Tower, killing six people, and injuring more than 1,000. Several nearby businesses, including the Vista International Hotel, were severely damaged. Because my office was located near my home in Princeton, New Jersey more than 50 miles away from the bombing, and because my focus was on navigating a fairly steep and time consuming learning curve while re-entering the investment business I had left in 1978, I paid only perfunctory attention to the incident.

However, news people never truly leave the news business. Poking around with my former journalism colleagues to learn more about bombing mastermind Sheik Amar Abdel-Rahman and his connection to terrorist Ramzi Yousef, my glaring ignorance of the history and specifics of Islam became apparent. Exacerbated by my need to make a living, like many New York-centric people, I regarded Abdel-Rahman, the blind sheik in Jersey City with the red-and-white Santa Claus hat as a nut-job, a dangerous murderer to be brought to justice. Because of my ignorance, I did not hold "his religious beliefs" against him.

The next five years were marked by an emersion into a Merrill Lynch culture which was between two worlds - the "anything goes" Wall Street excesses of the 1980's featuring lavish paid vacations at exotic locations - and the chastened world of the 1993-94 bond market meltdown, and later the onset of the "Asian Contagion" after the Thai baht was devalued. My 1990s experience at Merrill Lynch left me with the retrospective that I rarely met a member of that firm with whom I had worked I didn't like.

My obligatory five years at Merrill Lynch ended when I saw the writing on the wall suggesting that my mentor there would be leaving the firm. In 1998 I was recruited to the Smith Barney Branch Office in New Brunswick, New Jersey, home of my Alma Mater, Rutgers. My large corner office there overlooked the historic New Brunswick Train Station; the large signing bonus I received for moving my clientele alleviated the precarious financial condition in which the The Monitor Channel's destruction had left me; the ability to walk across the street to catch a train into New York was a delightful perk; the city's restaurants at the time were outstanding; occasionally strolling the lively Rutgers campus was always delightful; and the influence of Branch Manager Peter Lundgren, along with the group of Advisors he managed indicated I had made a good move. My son Zachary graduated in 1998 from UMASS after spending a semester in Switzerland, my two daughters were still in high school, and life was generally serendipitous.

The morning of Tuesday, September 1st, 2001 was a horrifying reminder of my ignorance regarding Islam. I had missed my train into New York for a client meeting and elected to duck into my office to make some calls and await the next train. "Turn on your TVs, turn on your TVs", shouted a terrified Christine, the office administrator, "there's been an accident"! As the screen illuminated, I declared aloud, "That's no accident: the worst pilot on the planet wouldn't let that happen". Immediately calling my wife, as we were talking about what appeared to be happening, the second plane struck. "Zach!" escaped our lips simultaneously. Our son, who had enlisted in the Marines three months earlier, was that very morning at Marines Corps Base Camp Lejeune receiving a meritorious award, and was scheduled to return to San Diego. Planes headed west were dropping from the sky. Our youngest daughter's high school was on lock-down protocol. Her older sister called from college, sobbing about her brother's predicament and the world in general. The markets were closed indefinitely. Land-line phone service was spotty. I could not get through to any Marine facility. The anxiety throughout my office- indeed all of Wall Street - was off the charts, as the death toll and horror of it all kept rising. My son finally got through by phone late in the afternoon, responding to my concern with: "Don't worry Dad, your baby boy is in arguably the safest place on the planet now – a Marine Corps base on FPCON (Force Protection Condition). It's unbelievable how amped up the guys getting deployed today are". I asked "What about you?". He said "I'm on lock-down for a while, don't know how long, but one thing I do know for sure: whoever did this is in deep shit".

Nightmares of young Marines going down in a hail of bullets or blown up by an I.E.D in some hell-hole abroad plagued my sleep for the next several years. The fatherly pride that had filled my heart and mind watching my son lead his company onto the historic

MCRD parade deck in San Diego on June 21st, 2001 swelled, but gave way to the sober realization that freedom isn't free, and that he had signed on to pay the ultimate price if necessary. I began paying attention to the notion of "radical Islam". Wanting to leapfrog agendized media reports, I bought a copy of the Quran with English translation to see what Islam was all about from the standpoint of Primary Document research. Imbedded among flowery passages of religiosity were many dogmatic, hate-driven calls for subjugation – even death – to those who chose a religious path different from Islam, i.e. "the infidels". Rooted out by research, my ignorance yielded to understanding. Also helpful during that time, one of my children worked at The White House under Homeland Security Counsel between 2005 and 2007.

This helped me recognize the media's avoidance of Islam, caliphates, and jihad. Discussions about Marxism and communist ideology were not yet fashionable in the press, so parallels drawn between any similarities was unusual. The library, and conversations with scholars, were necessary. I learned some interesting things. To wit:

The word "Caliph", precisely translated from the Arabic word "Khalifa" means "successor", denoting he who is the successor to the Prophet Muhammad. It has a close secondary translation meaning of "ruler" or "leader".

A "Caliphate" is defined as a form of government under Islamic law. Eight known caliphates have appeared since the Rashidun Caliphate immediately following the death of the Prophet Muhammed in 632 AD (CE for revisionists). All have attempted to create a unified Islamic governance. Both the Abbasid Caliphate, established in Baghdad between 750 – 1258 (and continued in Cairo until1517), and The Ottoman Caliphate each lasted more than a few centuries each. The Ottoman Caliphate (1517 and 1924) was abolished by the Turkish Republic in 1924, becoming the last of the widely recognized caliphates. The Islamic State (ISIS) Caliphate, which began in 2014, ended militarily in 2019. It is said to have lacked legitimacy among most Muslims.

The literal English translation of "Intifada" from the Arabic, is "shaking off". In recent years intifada has specifically defined a Palestinian uprising and resistance designed to end Israeli control over what Palestinians regard as Palestinian territories, and to create an independent Palestinian state. There have been two such intifadas: the first, begun in December 1987, ended in September 1993 with the signing of the Oslo Accords, a framework for peace negotiations between Israel and the Palestinians. The second intifada began in September 2000, and never really ended, but more accurately hit a lull by late 2005. Some 5000 Palestinians and 1400 Israelis died during these intifadas, characterized by suicide bombings and retaliations. In 2002, one particularly deadly suicide bombing killed 30, prompting the Israeli military to reoccupy the West Bank and parts of Gaza, for security. Hamas, which rejected the Oslo Accords, gained political control of Gaza in 2006 through legislative elections, and took power by force in Gaza in 2007. On October 7th, 2023, Hamas perpetrated a savage massacre, to which Israel responded with intense military operations in Gaza, and against Hezbollah in Southern Lebanon.

The Islamic Republic of Iran, in addition to sponsoring numerous other acts of terrorism in the region through proxies, reportedly supported both terrorist groups, and others.

Iran, which had overthrown the Shah (King) in 1979, had formed what it called an "Islamic Republic", installing the radical Islamic cleric-politician-revolutionary Ayatollah Khomeini as its founder and leader. There is a distinction between a caliphate and an Islamic Republic, but to many, it's a distinction without a difference, as both are based on Islamic law. Hidden behind the sophistry of Islam and Islamic culture stands one inescapable feature: Muslims can't seem to agree on who should be in charge. The long-time bellicose divide between Shia and Sunni sects continues. Among the Shia, efforts by Iran and its proxies to unite against and destroy the very existence of Israel and America - indeed ALL infidels - persist. The religious precepts of Islam, imbedded in Iran's politics, have made of Iran an enemy of Western civilization. In 2025, Iran became a vastly weakened enemy.

Comparisons of Communism and Islam are compelling. Marxism is a much newer, but no less deadly belief system than Islam. It was promulgated by Karl Marx and Friedrich Engels in 1848 Europe, with publication of their <u>Communist Manifesto</u> in London. Unlike Islam, which is a monotheistic religion, the communist ideologist Marx famously regarded religion as "The opiate of the masses", regarding it as a tool used by capitalists to further inequality. His views of oppressor vs oppressed classes in 19th century Europe led him to predict and even promote the use of violent revolution in order for "oppressed" classes to overthrow their capitalist "oppressors". Islam's "Death to Israel", "Death to America" "Death to Infidels" tracks pretty closely to Joseph Stalin's "Death is the solution to all problems. No man, no problem". China's Mao Zedong focused on eliminating (murdering) enemies of his "cultural revolution" through purges, justifying his extreme measures, including mass executions, with slogans such as "When there is not enough to eat people starve to death. It is better to let half the people die so that the other half can eat their fill". The Chinese Communist Party (CCP) is officially atheist, and its members are not permitted to join any religion.

My religious research since 9/11 has synthesized and expanded my appreciation of how The Daycroft Factor had shaped my consciousness during my early formation. While having grasped the continuum of Judaism and genuine Christianity while growing up, I had as an adult felt compelled to learn enough facts about what I came to regard as the defective religion of Islam: that it by doctrine encourages willful, hateful harm, including death, to those who reject it. At the same time, I recognized that the human governance of "The Christian

Science Church" had succeeded in burying the beneficial truths of Christian Science in a series of "mistakes" since 1910, perhaps based on misapprehension, perhaps more nefarious than that. Islam, on the other hand, hid its dysfunctions in plain sight.

On Friday, July 21st, 2006, Smith Barney Branch Manager Peter Lundgren died suddenly, but not unexpectedly, as he had suffered several heart attacks previously and showed little interest in moderating his lifestyle, which included his affection for wine and pleasures of the table. Peter was fundamentally a very good man, and I learned much about how the world works from Peter, who elevated my understanding of the markets. I had no desire or intention to wait around for his replacement, whose expertise and understanding of Wall Street would be unlikely to replicate Peter's. As a result, I accepted a recruiting offer from Morgan Stanley, where I intended to spend the rest of my Wall Street Career.

Morgan Stanley had subsequently acquired Smith Barney during the historic capital markets meltdown beginning in 2008, and I finished my career on Wall Street at Morgan Stanley in 2023. In addition to making many interesting new friends, my 50 years in the capital markets provided numerous opportunities to utilize all of the attributes I had acquired during my 12 years at Daycroft, allowing me to make a good living, allowing me the opportunity to support my family well, so that my children could develop their talents with the uncompromised and unconditional parental support of a mother who devoted her primary attention and boundless energies to their development. My wife Judy, a bright and spectacularly pleasant person, had run for mayoralty office in the growing Township of South Brunswick New Jersey in the 1980s, served on its Planning and Zoning boards, Environmental Commission, was active in the PTA, and devoted what time she had left to real estate and other part-time compensatory work. However, it has never ceased to amaze me that her primary exemplary work for some thirty years was as

Managing Director of our family's home, a calling which successfully launched our three very accomplished children.

When previously returning to the actual world of money and markets after leaving broadcasting, I was forced to parlay my proven communication skills, a large network of friends, former business associates, and television acquaintances in order to rise from the ashes of my broadcasting career, torched by The Monitor Channel's destruction As I turned my prior unique experiences into a successful outcome, it became more and more clear to me, even as I hit several personal speed bumps, that The Daycroft Factor was giving me a certain view of the world decidedly different than many episodes in my adult life had presented. Many of the clients I developed not only thought of me as a trusted friend and advisor for financial affairs, but in matters of family and other personal issues as well. To my relief and delight, every one of those I had regarded as good clients moved their accounts with me when I was recruited first to Smith Barney, and later to Morgan Stanley. Some have since jokingly refused to allow me to retire, and they remain good friends with whom I speak regularly.

Portfolio Management

To all persons, let it be known that

William Dredge

has completed the prescribed studies and satisfied the requirements for the Portfolio Management program at Morgan Stanley Smith Barney.

October 18, 2011

MorganStanley
SmithBarney

Throughout my careers, encompassing as they did the homely succession of sacrifice and toils with which all fathers worthy of the name are familiar, and by which human life is transmitted, it became more and more clear that successful things in life are first driven by moral and spiritual considerations, and then economic ones, *in that order*. In particular, as my son finished his tour with the Marines, I increasingly studied whenever possible the continuum involving the 5,000 years of history between Judaism and Christianity, pondering the divide between the two, and I continued to correct my ignorance of Islam. It would not be until 2025 that I began to draw parallels between the eight caliphates of Islam beginning in 632 AD (CE for revisionists) and Marxism, which began its own metastasis in 1848.

On Saturday evening June 20th, 2025, while attending the wedding of two young Navy Medical Corpsmen, I learned of the successful United States Air Force mission setting Iran's nuclear weapons program back indefinitely. In the days since, the press tossed around words like "caliphate" and "intifada", in clear indication that the Fourth Estate is indeed in some form of foreclosure, or should be. Punctuating the cacophony, a few days later a Muslim communist running as a democrat won a primary election in New York City, winning the New York City Mayoralty by a wide margin. It occurred to me that at a minimum, some definitional clarity was in order.

I recall reflecting often over the years on the fact that our children had been introduced to the disparate benefits of two Christian denominations – the beauty of Roman Catholic ritualism, and the metaphysical precepts of Christian Science. Because of this, and because both ways of life are theoretically based on common spiritual precepts, my wife and I had come to a very comfortable and elevating ecumenical understanding regarding the business of religion. Once, in a conversation during a long drive back from a weekend getaway, my dear wife recited a quote attributed to Napolean Bonapart: "Sweetheart, don't you understand that 'the sole purpose of organized religion is to keep the poor from killing the rich'"?

While I found her contribution to our conversation humorous, it was a quotation that became entirely comprehensible to me, a man whose early religious formation, and careers in journalism and Wall Street had revealed that money and religion do not mix well. My deeper investigation at that time of both Islam and Marxism gave support to that assessment. It has become increasingly clear to me that mankind's abandonment of spiritual precepts and/or confusion about them, produces problems – some cataclysmic.

In December of 2008, my dear father-in-law John Rosta had passed from this earth. The love and care demonstrated by his family and faith community had moved me deeply. A robust and active man until the stroke that took him out, I was honored to eulogize him at Saint Ladislaus church, noting his own consecration to Christ. The packed congregation of friends and family, who turned out on what had to have been the coldest day of the year, was deeply moving to me. When I finished my eulogy, I turned to offer a polite head bow to the iconic image of Jesus on the cross, and noted Father Polgar wiping tears from his eyes. As I stepped down from the chancel, my wife's older brother rose from his seat, strode thirty feet or so, and tearfully shook my hand, thanking me. The funeral cortege to the nearby burial site was miles long, and the bugle's sad refrain of "Taps", played under a clear blue noonday sky by a gentleman of the Army, signaled the passing of an era. During the repast which followed, my desire to honor both my parents' sacrifices to send me to Daycroft, and my father-in-law's own consecration to Christ, were renewed.

With my wife as my sponsor, I interviewed with Father Polgar at the Saint Ladislaus rectory a few days later, to share my assessment of "right religion, wrong church". At the end of that long interview, Father Polgar declared, "Mr. Dredge, you know more than most priests do". Shortly thereafter, bypassing the traditional Order of Christian Initiation by which adults are usually joined with the Catholic church, I received the Rite of Recognition, welcoming me into membership. At my age 12, my mother's sincere desire to enroll me in the Boston-based Christian Science church had been well-intended. Her sudden passing 12 years later, in 1970, likely precluded any awareness she had of things I later learned about that organization. I concluded that she would have understood, if not entirely approved of my dual membership in both churches, had she lived to endure what became known to me, and others, after she left us.

At one point in 2011, a watershed event brought me face-to-face with just how shallow and one-dimensional my human journey in Wall Street had become. An excruciatingly painful, nearly debilitating back pain problem had resulted in a prescription for therapeutic massage. The lovely Asian-American massage therapist assigned to me by the health club of which I had been a member for 25 years eventually decided to accept my offer to work on me at my home each week. That way, I had reasoned, she could keep the full amount I was paying to the club for her services, plus a little more. Knowing her financial circumstances, I bought a massage table and everything she might need for her work in my home, so she wouldn't have to lug her own equipment to and from each week. I paid her well, and treated her like a member of the family. She was able to breeze in on Thursday evenings and help heal my back issues. My wife liked her, and I was totally oblivious to the professional conflicts with which she struggled as our relationship continued over five years. While nothing sexually untoward ever happened between us, the relationship became untenably close, ending because of moral and ethical factors I had learned about so many years earlier, but had abandoned while pursuing worldly wealth in Wall Street. While her abrupt departure was puzzling and emotionally very disquieting, the dissolution of our relationship provided an opportunity for reflection and invited reform, affecting every aspect of my life. I lost 70 pounds on purpose within the six months that followed. Each subsequent stage of transformation unearthed elements of the Daycroft Factor buried under years of subconscious denial, suppressed spirituality, and an ambivalence toward divine Principle and Truth. I came face-to-face with the allure of hedonistic appetites and tendencies; and I began the prodigal revaluation of the homely succession of sacrifices and toils which fortunate humans endure as they journey through life. For the first time since graduating from Rutgers in 1971, the idealistic desire to make the world a little better than I had found it, was rekindled.

CASA for Children of Mercer and Burlington Counties
Certificate of Training

This is to certify that

William Dredge

Has successfully completed training for appointment as a

Court Appointed Special Advocate
To represent the best interests of abused and neglected children

Awarded this 3rd day of April, 2013.

Lori V. Morris
Executive Director

I began to sneak off at lunchtime to take honors history courses at a nearby college. Training at night for six months to become a volunteer Court Appointed Special Advocate (CASA) for children in foster care removed from their homes due to abuse, my eyes were opened to the needs and rights of others from markedly impoverished backgrounds. I learned firsthand the plight of the urban poor in cities like Trenton New Jersey, and elsewhere, whose lot in life was entirely different than that of my Wall Street colleagues and clients. In one case to which I was assigned, I was able to help a mother of four children, each fathered by a different man, escape from the alcohol, drug abuse, gang activity, prostitution and other maladies by which she had been enslaved. Including her in my advocacy for her teen-aged son in court, (a departure from the practice generally observed by CASAs), I took her under my wing, helped her regain visitation rights with her son, one of the four children previously removed from her home, helped her obtain legal aid, bought her an air conditioner for an apartment she was able to rent in the Projects, advocated in court for her son to be able to move in with her when he aged out of the system; and I still get a phone call from them from time to time, keeping me up to date, and expressing appreciation. It was one of many cases which returned the salutary clarity of The Daycroft Factor, renewing a sense of purpose, deep satisfaction and joy which giving kindness without expecting anything in return can bring to human existence. I learned empirically that this satisfaction and joy cannot be bought with money.

EPILOGUE

What I have broadly labeled "The Daycroft Factor" has integrated in my consciousness the quality of thought describing genuine Christian Science attending my journey over the past seven decades or so. It can for those of good will be quite helpful in every aspect of human existence, and elements of it sometimes are, by other names. The Daycroft Factor itself has suffered the slings and arrows of human organization since barely surviving the closing of the Daycroft School. This begs some questions: have world conditions in general improved since then? Do students graduating from elementary and high schools – even colleges today - read, write or understand math and science better? Has addiction to drugs, alcohol, and any other addictions enslaving too many people been mitigated? Has the insidious process of inflation been successfully addressed and remedied? Has domestic violence, indeed violence as the dispute resolution *du jour*, diminished? Are there fewer wars in the world? Questions regarding a wide range of disorders abound. The Daycroft Factor provides fertile soil for demonstrable answers, once perceived. It requires the nourishment of constructive thought and activity, a sincere desire for improvement in all aspects of the human condition, and a courageous willingness to "Perceive Then Demonstrate" through action to cultivate this fertile soil.

It is instructively emblematic to me that women in the 19th century were widely regarded as chattel (as they are today in some parts of the world). That changed in 1920 in the United States with ratification of the 19th Amendment of the U.S. Constitution, although some women continued to face significant barriers to exercising their right to vote until 1965. Indeed, discouragements, subtle and overt, continue to thwart all manner of enlightenment and reform throughout planet earth for so many. It is clear that, undismayed by arguably worse problems in her time, an inspired thinker of the 19th century, Mary Baker Eddy, had worked with tireless energy to complete her seminal textbook <u>Science and Health with Key to the Scriptures, Prose Works and Miscellaneous Writings</u>, later publishing her <u>Christian Science Journal,</u> and other periodicals. Persuaded by thousands of her followers, who had reportedly felt the need for physical structures in which to enjoy congregational worship, she authorized the building of a magnificent cathedral in Boston, in which she never set foot. But her most prescient contribution to secular thought came in 1908, with the publication of The Christian Science Monitor. This achievement gained her widespread worldly admiration and acclaim among those of good will around the world. <u>The Christian Science Monitor</u> was NOT a religious publication. By 1908, the stench of so-called "yellow journalism" permeated the newspaper business. <u>The Monitor</u> brought a much needed breath of fresh air to the dissemination of news and information to the public at that time. Despite its relatively small size and reach, it gained a well-deserved reputation for clean, fair, and comprehensive journalism, bringing truthful insights to readers, establishing it as a world-class newspaper, even for those who cursed her, and the genuine Christian Science which she had articulated to the world earlier. Today, in the wake of an institutional departure from her clear vision, <u>The Christian Science Monitor</u> no longer exists as a daily printed newspaper. Equally as sad, "Club C.S." had helped destroy The Monitor Channel in its infancy, surrendering the marketplace of ideas to a vast proliferation of alternate technologies, which may someday resurrect the publication's mission *"To injure no man, but to bless all mankind"*, which had echoed throughout its history. The generation of financial resources necessary to stand out among these technologies now rests upon a strategy of using the real estate of The Mother Church, The First Church of Christ, Scientist, in Boston Massachusetts, to generate revenue, along with written solicitations to branch churches with dwindling memberships, and to individuals.

While reviewing these things since retiring from Morgan Stanley in 2023, I came upon the following, which prompted my needed recognition of, and encouragement toward the moral, ethical, and spiritual constructs which The Daycroft Factor inspires. The New Testament's book of Revelation, said to be authored by the apostle John, was as much a topic of theological controversy and interpretation in the 19th century as it has been since the inception of the early Church some two millennia previously, and to this very day. In her seminal textbook Science and Health with Key to the Scriptures, Mrs. Eddy gives her thoughts on Revelation xii. 15,16:

"Millions of unprejudiced minds – simple seekers for Truth, weary wanderers, athirst in the desert – are waiting and watching for rest and drink. Give them a cup of cold water in Christ's name, and never fear the consequences. What if the old dragon should send forth a new flood to drown the Christ-idea? He can neither drown your voice with its roar, or again sink the world into the deep waters of chaos and old night".

Like the stately oak tree which once stood on an open field in Stamford Connecticut depicted on the former Daycroft School's emblem, The Daycroft Factor is nourished by natural nutrients, by sunlight following the dawn, alertness to and active protection from harmful elements as it grows; it provides abundant shade and encourages rest beneath it branches to weary students seeking the trinity of Life, Truth, and Love; and, like the firewood it provides after the tree itself has run its course, The Daycroft Factor provides warm comfort and inspiration in winter's long cold nights, inspiration including the desire to "Perceive then Demonstrate" daily to the best of one's desire and ability. In retrospect, and previously often unacknowledged by me, it has made all the difference in my life. I humbly and respectfully offer it as a beacon of light, a sovereign panacea for all who yearn to bring healing to a world so greatly in need of it.

ABOUT THE AUTHOR

William B. Dredge has always had a burning desire to honor his parents' sacrifices in sending him to The Daycroft School, a small private school in Connecticut for 12 years of his primary and secondary education. That desire remains kindled by the morals and ethics permeating the educational atmosphere influencing him at Daycroft, which encouraged spiritual enlightenment, fellowship, leadership, and productive activity. These qualities had allowed him to become an award-winning pioneer as a journalist in business and financial news on television, encompassing more than a decade anchoring for The Wall Street Journal and the Christian Science Monitor. Returning to the brass knuckle world of Wall Street in 1993, he parlayed his journalism career into productive accomplishments at Merrill Lynch, Smith Barney and Morgan Stanley during the tumultuously turbulent 30 years since then, with insights gained not only serving clients of those firms, but with *pro bono* civic activities, including serving as a Court Appointed Special Advocate for children in foster care removed from their homes because of abuse.

In 2024, he returned to his first love, writing, memorializing some of his unusual life experiences since 1951. Bill and his wife Judy have three grown children and seven grandchildren. Presented through the prism of clear-eyed spiritual discernment, tempered by 50 years in and around the capital markets, punctuated with moments of sometimes hilarious episodes and serious insights, he credits a life well lived to what he has coined <u>The Daycroft Factor.</u>

www.ingramcontent.com/pod-product-compliance
Lightning Source LLC
Chambersburg PA
CBHW041627140626
46547CB00031B/1110